I0429217

LEBANON'S SECURITY CHALLENGES AND U.S. INTERESTS

HEARING

BEFORE THE

SUBCOMMITTEE ON
THE MIDDLE EAST AND NORTH AFRICA

OF THE

COMMITTEE ON FOREIGN AFFAIRS
HOUSE OF REPRESENTATIVES

ONE HUNDRED THIRTEENTH CONGRESS

SECOND SESSION

APRIL 8, 2014

Serial No. 113–133

Printed for the use of the Committee on Foreign Affairs

Available via the World Wide Web: http://www.foreignaffairs.house.gov/ or
http://www.gpo.gov/fdsys/

U.S. GOVERNMENT PRINTING OFFICE

87–514PDF   WASHINGTON : 2014

For sale by the Superintendent of Documents, U.S. Government Printing Office
Internet: bookstore.gpo.gov   Phone: toll free (866) 512–1800; DC area (202) 512–1800
Fax: (202) 512–2104   Mail: Stop IDCC, Washington, DC 20402–0001

COMMITTEE ON FOREIGN AFFAIRS

EDWARD R. ROYCE, California, *Chairman*

CHRISTOPHER H. SMITH, New Jersey
ILEANA ROS-LEHTINEN, Florida
DANA ROHRABACHER, California
STEVE CHABOT, Ohio
JOE WILSON, South Carolina
MICHAEL T. McCAUL, Texas
TED POE, Texas
MATT SALMON, Arizona
TOM MARINO, Pennsylvania
JEFF DUNCAN, South Carolina
ADAM KINZINGER, Illinois
MO BROOKS, Alabama
TOM COTTON, Arkansas
PAUL COOK, California
GEORGE HOLDING, North Carolina
RANDY K. WEBER SR., Texas
SCOTT PERRY, Pennsylvania
STEVE STOCKMAN, Texas
RON DeSANTIS, Florida
DOUG COLLINS, Georgia
MARK MEADOWS, North Carolina
TED S. YOHO, Florida
LUKE MESSER, Indiana

ELIOT L. ENGEL, New York
ENI F.H. FALEOMAVAEGA, American
   Samoa
BRAD SHERMAN, California
GREGORY W. MEEKS, New York
ALBIO SIRES, New Jersey
GERALD E. CONNOLLY, Virginia
THEODORE E. DEUTCH, Florida
BRIAN HIGGINS, New York
KAREN BASS, California
WILLIAM KEATING, Massachusetts
DAVID CICILLINE, Rhode Island
ALAN GRAYSON, Florida
JUAN VARGAS, California
BRADLEY S. SCHNEIDER, Illinois
JOSEPH P. KENNEDY III, Massachusetts
AMI BERA, California
ALAN S. LOWENTHAL, California
GRACE MENG, New York
LOIS FRANKEL, Florida
TULSI GABBARD, Hawaii
JOAQUIN CASTRO, Texas

AMY PORTER, *Chief of Staff*   THOMAS SHEEHY, *Staff Director*
JASON STEINBAUM, *Democratic Staff Director*

––––––––

SUBCOMMITTEE ON THE MIDDLE EAST AND NORTH AFRICA

ILEANA ROS-LEHTINEN, Florida, *Chairman*

STEVE CHABOT, Ohio
JOE WILSON, South Carolina
ADAM KINZINGER, Illinois
TOM COTTON, Arkansas
RANDY K. WEBER SR., Texas
RON DeSANTIS, Florida
DOUG COLLINS, Georgia
MARK MEADOWS, North Carolina
TED S. YOHO, Florida
LUKE MESSER, Indiana

THEODORE E. DEUTCH, Florida
GERALD E. CONNOLLY, Virginia
BRIAN HIGGINS, New York
DAVID CICILLINE, Rhode Island
ALAN GRAYSON, Florida
JUAN VARGAS, California
BRADLEY S. SCHNEIDER, Illinois
JOSEPH P. KENNEDY III, Massachusetts
GRACE MENG, New York
LOIS FRANKEL, Florida

CONTENTS

LEBANON'S SECURITY CHALLENGES AND U.S. INTERESTS

TUESDAY, APRIL 8, 2014

HOUSE OF REPRESENTATIVES,
SUBCOMMITTEE ON THE MIDDLE EAST AND NORTH AFRICA,
COMMITTEE ON FOREIGN AFFAIRS,
Washington, DC.

The committee met, pursuant to notice, at 10 o'clock a.m., in room 2172 Rayburn House Office Building, Hon. Ileana Ros-Lehtinen (chairman of the subcommittee) presiding.

Ms. ROS-LEHTINEN. Well, thank you very much. The subcommittee will come to order.

Afer recognizing myself and Ranking Member Ted Deutch for 5 minutes each for our opening statements, I will then recognize other members seeking recognition for 1 minute. We will then hear from our witnesses and without objection the witnesses' prepared statements will be made a part of the record and members may have 5 days to insert questions and statements for the record subject to the length limitations in the rules.

And there are several committees that are meeting at the same time including where Attorney General Holder is testifying so we are bouncing back and forth from committee. So we apologize if it seems to be sparsely attended. They will come back and forth.

The chair now recognizes herself for 5 minutes. Lebanon is a country that is seemingly perpetually in a state of conflict or on the verge of breaking out into conflict at any moment.

A bloody and protracted civil war ravaged the country over 25 years ago and Lebanon has never really been quite able to fully recover. One of the by-products of the Lebanese civil war was the emergence of Hezbollah in the early 1980s.

Long associated with the Ba'ath Party in Syria led by Bashar al-Assad and his father before him and backed by the Iranian regime, Hezbollah has received its financial and military support from Tehran while allying itself politically with Damascus.

Hezbollah is a U.S. designated terrorist organization and has been responsible for conducting many acts of violence that have left hundreds of innocent U.S. and Israeli citizens dead.

It has long waged a war against our closest friend and ally, the democratic Jewish State of Israel, most notably setting off the 2006 conflict when it conducted a cross border raid in Israel, kidnapping and killing Israeli soldiers.

This led to a 34-day-long campaign in which Hezbollah fired thousands of rockets indiscriminately into Israel, prompting an

(1)

Israeli military response that finally ended in a cease fire. Now we see Hezbollah responsible for much of the bloodshed in Syria and it has brought that conflict across the border into Lebanon and with it other terrorist groups like al-Qaeda-linked Islamic State of Iraq and the Levant, ISIL.

This is not just a threat for Lebanon. This increased violence threatens to destabilize the entire region, threatening U.S. national interests and our democratic partner, Israel.

In recent months, ISIL has been seeking to expand its influence in Lebanon and its commander said the group would use Lebanon as a gateway for al-Qaeda to strike Israel.

So how do we protect U.S. security interest or Israel and ensure stability in Lebanon? The strain that the Syrian conflict has put on Lebanon cannot be understated. Last week, the U.N. high commissioner for refugees announced that the number of refugees who have fled to Lebanon is now over 1 million and counting.

The United States continues to provide humanitarian assistance to Lebanon, nearly $350 million to date, in an effort to help it cope with this massive influx of refugees, and since 2006 we have also increased our security assistance to Lebanon with the goal of improving the capacity of Lebanese Armed Forces, LAF, and its Internal Security Forces, ISF, aiming to bolster their capacity to serve as effective and nonsectarian forces to provide safety in Lebanon.

Lebanon is in the middle of a political transition, again divided along religious ideologies and positions taken in support or against Assad in Syria, and it is imperative that a government can be formed that can put aside sectarian and religious identities and work toward stabilizing the country. A small step was taken earlier this year when a new cabinet was formed after nearly a year of deadlocked negotiations.

But now with the current President's term set to expire next month and elections pushed back until November, continued violence and animosity between the main political groups threatens to derail the process. The administration must continue to press the Lebanese leaders to hold free, fair and transparent elections on time.

But in order to have elections, the security situation must improve so we must help the LAF and the ISF fight back the increased sectarian violence that is tearing the country apart. The U.S. cannot continue to take a reactive lead-from-behind approach in Lebanon as it has been doing throughout the rest of the region.

The administration's failed policies in Syria and Iran did not create the atmosphere we see in Lebanon now but they have certainly contributed to the instability.

Instead of coddling Iran and offering concession after concession, we should be condemning the Iranian regime for its support of terrorism, namely Hezbollah, and its abysmal human rights record.

Even while the Syrian crisis continues and the sectarian violence spreads throughout Lebanon, we cannot forget that these terror groups continue to pose a very real threat to U.S. national security and to Israel.

Just last month Israel seized an Iranian arms shipment that was headed to Gaza and likely bound for Hezbollah and Israel continues to see the Assad regime attempt to transport sophisticated weapons like Russian-supplied surface to air missiles to these extremists and Israel is then forced to take action to prevent these transfers.

It is time that the administration defines a clear and decisive plan and takes real and concrete action to defend our interest and that of our allies.

And with that, I turn to our ranking member, Mr. Deutch.

Mr. DEUTCH. Thank you, Madame Chairman. Thank you, Deputy Assistant Secretary Silverman and Spence for being here today. I think we all agree that Lebanon is truly at a critical juncture and has increased the tension for the United States and from the international community.

Lebanon has faced tremendous internal struggles, from a 15-year civil war to foreign intervention to its balancing act with Hezbollah functioning as a de facto state within a state, and now these initial struggles are compounded by the increasing external pressures of regional events.

Perhaps no country in the region has been as adversely affected by the Syrian crisis as Lebanon. Last week the United Nations registered the millionth Syrian refugee in Lebanon—over 1 million Syrians officially now refugees in a country whose population is only 4 million.

With no official refugee camps, Syrians are now in 1,600 different towns and cities desperately looking for work and shelter. The humanitarian effect of the Syrian crisis on Lebanon is only one piece of the puzzle.

Spillover from the feud between the Assad-aligned Hezbollah fighters and al-Qaeda-affiliated extremists has dramatically increased violence on the ground in Lebanon. Retaliatory bombings have struck both Sunni and Shi'ite areas and targeted Lebanese armed forces and security services personnel.

Hezbollah is so deeply ingrained into the fabric of Lebanese society that Shi'ite populations have no choice but to rely on it not just for security but for social services, schools and health care. A legitimate Lebanese Government cannot function effectively when it is in a constant power struggle to govern with a nonstate actor.

But calling itself a resistance movement or a political party does not diminish from what Hezbollah truly is—an Iranian-backed worldwide terrorist organization. Hezbollah's activities have destabilized the entire region from its estimated 4,000 fighters in Syria to its recent cross border attack on an IDF convoy. Hezbollah has launched attacks around the globe and every single day has 75,000 rockets aimed at Israel.

Hezbollah's illicit financing ventures have propelled it to a global criminal network with fundraising and finance operations in Europe, in Africa and in Latin America.

I commend my colleagues on this committee—Brad Schneider and Mark Meadows along with Chairman Royce and Ranking Member Engel—for the introduction of new legislation that will help the United States rein in Hezbollah's illicit activities and financing of terrorism around the globe.

Deputy Assistant Secretary Silverman, I hope that you will speak to what more the U.S. can do to strengthen actors that can provide a viable alternative to Hezbollah. The selection of a new

President who is beholden to Hezbollah would greatly diminish efforts to ensure the Lebanese Armed Forces have sole responsibility for the country's security.

At the same time, the LAF must be held accountable by the U.S. and our partners for this charge, meaning the LAF must treat all security threats whether from Hezbollah or al-Qaeda outlying militias the same.

I am concerned about reports that many feel the LAF is losing its neutrality due to its hesitancy to provoke Hezbollah. The U.S. has engaged in training the LAF in the areas of border control and counterterrorism and Lebanon receives the fourth largest sum of U.S. international military training and education funds.

We must encourage our Western and regional partners to continue to support the Lebanese Armed Forces. This includes international enforcement of Security Council Resolution 1701, which calls for the disarmament of all armed groups in Lebanon and gives full security control to the forces of the Lebanese Government.

Saudi Arabia committed $3 billion in military aid to Lebanon. We must work in concert with the French and our partners in the International Support Group for Lebanon to ensure that these finds are delivered in an effective manner.

Improving the immediate security situation is a first step toward repairing the Lebanese economy. Significant pressure from the influx of Syrian refugees has led to a total economic loss to the country of $7.5 billion from 2012 to 2014, according to World Bank estimates.

Official unemployment is at 20 percent. Significant energy finds may also contribute to Lebanon's long-term financial stability but it is imperative that any potential exploration follows only after a settlement to the maritime border dispute in the eastern Mediterranean.

As the U.S. continues to provide humanitarian assistance to address the immediate needs of Lebanon, we must also consider investing in long-term projects that can shore up Lebanon's economy for years to come.

Madam Chairman, Lebanon cannot maintain its balancing act forever and I fear we are reaching the tipping point. Now is the time to increase pressure on Hezbollah and increase support for government institutions to help steer Lebanon on a path to stability and true democracy.

I thank you and I yield back.

Ms. ROS-LEHTINEN. Thank you, Mr. Deutch. Excellent opening statement, and we have three members who have indicated that they are the ones who would like to have 1-minute opening statements and we are thrilled that they do want to do so.

So Mr. Meadows of North Carolina, whose bill is related to Hezbollah. Thank you.

Mr. MEADOWS. Thank you, Madam Chairman. Thank you both for coming here. It is good to see you again, Mr. Silverman. I look forward to hearing your testimony on how we from a policy standpoint can best implement policy to help the Lebanese people enjoy a peaceful and secure environment.

Obviously, our ally, Israel, right next door has tens of thousands if not hundreds of thousands of rockets aimed at them from many of the Hezbollah-related activities.

We have introduced as recent as yesterday a sanctioning bill and would like to hear your comments on that how that might be effective, how we could potentially adjust that to make it an effective tool for the administration to address many of the terrorist activities that we all have come to know and read about on a regular basis.

So I look forward to your testimony and I yield back, Madam Chair.

Ms. ROS-LEHTINEN. Thank you, Mr. Meadows. Mr. Schneider of Illinois.

Mr. SCHNEIDER. Thank you, Madam Chair and Ranking Member Deutch, for convening this timely hearing. Thank you to the witnesses for being here today.

Lebanon is at a precipice, facing the specter of renewed sectarian strife fueled by the civil war in Syria. Over 1 million refugees have crossed the border, putting extreme pressure on Lebanon's already stretched resources.

At the same time, Hezbollah fighters are active in Syria, fighting on behalf of the Assad regime, while Sunni extremists are increasingly active inside Lebanon. It is in this context that the U.S. must understand the dynamics of the challenges in Lebanon and develop intelligent policy to protect our interests and security and the security of our allies in the region.

In that vein, yesterday I was pleased to join my friend, Mark Meadows, Chairman Royce and Ranking Member Engel to introduce legislation targeting Hezbollah's global financing, drug trafficking and propaganda programs.

Hezbollah's activities threaten not just peace and stability in Lebanon but throughout the region, in particular our key ally, Israel. The Hezbollah International Financing Prevention Act would provide the administration with a strong enforcement mechanism to combat Hezbollah's terrorist financing that is destabilizing throughout the Middle East.

I look forward to hearing from our witnesses on how best to address this global financial network and what tools we can provide the administration to help go after these illegal networks.

Thank you, and I yield back.

Ms. ROS-LEHTINEN. Thank you, Mr. Schneider. Mr. Higgins of New York.

Mr. HIGGINS. Thank you, Madam Chair.

You know, Lebanon is a microcosm of, I think, the general problem that we deal with in the Middle East. It is highly pluralistic. It has a history of civil war over 15 years. It was probably the first minority-led regime in the Middle East behind Iraq and currently Syria.

Hezbollah, Party of God, is a Shi'a organization bent on violent jihad. They act as a proxy for Iran, Syria and Venezuela. They have a presence in North America, including 15 American cities.

They have about 60,000 missiles, medium and long range, and they sit at the northern border of Israel. Getting Lebanon right but also recognizing that America's role in this is going to be very, very limited and we have got to find a way to influence it without getting entangled in it, which I think is the larger problem that we deal with in the Middle East.

So with that, I will yield back the balance of my time and look forward to the testimony.

Ms. ROS-LEHTINEN. Thank you very much, Mr. Higgins, and thank you to all of our members.

I am very pleased to introduce our witnesses. First, we welcome Mr. Lawrence Silverman, who is Deputy Assistant Secretary of State for Near Eastern Affairs at the Department of State.

Prior to this position, Mr. Silverman was director of Israel and Palestinian Affairs and focused primarily on the Middle East, serving overseas in Jordan and Syria and in Washington as special advisor to Assistant Secretary of Near Eastern Affairs, William Burns.

Mr. Silverman began his State Department career in South Africa and Namibia where he was a member of the U.S. team that negotiated the agreement leading to the independence of that country and the withdrawal of Cuban troops from Angola. Job well done.

We also have with us, and we thank him for being here, Dr. Matthew Spence, who was appointed Deputy Assistant Secretary of Defense for Middle East policy in February 2012. Prior to joining the Defense Department, Dr. Spence served as special assistant to the president and senior director for international economic affairs at the National Security Council, and from '09 to '11 he was senior advisor to the national security advisor at the White House.

Thank you very much, both of you gentlemen, for joining us, and Mr. Silverman, we will begin with you.

STATEMENT OF MR. LAWRENCE SILVERMAN, DEPUTY ASSIST-ANT SECRETARY, BUREAU OF NEAR EASTERN AFFAIRS, U.S. DEPARTMENT OF STATE

Mr. SILVERMAN. Thank you very much, Chairman Ros-Lehtinen, Ranking Member Deutch, distinguished——

Ms. ROS-LEHTINEN. You could put the microphone a little bit closer.

Mr. SILVERMAN. Is that better? Thank you very much, Chairman Ros-Lehtinen and Ranking Member Deutch, distinguished members of the subcommittee.

Thank you for inviting me to testify on Lebanon, a country whose stability is central to U.S. interest in the region.

This is a key moment for Lebanon. The massive refugee influx, the largest per capita in the world, is an urgent humanitarian crisis. Lebanon, as you say, just registered its 1-millionth Syrian refugee, representing over 20 percent of its population.

Lebanon faces rising security and economic challenges. The United States is responding to these challenges because we want a stable secure Lebanese partner. In the midst of these challenges, Lebanon's political leaders have passed two of three political hurdles this year.

The March 20 approval of Prime Minister Salam's cabinet after months of stalemate is welcome. So is the government's agreement on a ministerial statement and a vote of confidence that empowers it to address all issues, unlike its predecessor.

The government includes eight members from the March 14 coalition, eight members from the March 8 coalition and eight others without formal affiliation. It is an improvement over its predecessor in that nearly all factions are represented in a careful balance. How we will work with the government depends on its policies and its actions.

President Suleiman's term in office is scheduled to end on May 25th. United States strongly believes that Presidential elections, the third hurdle, should be conducted on time, freely and fairly and without foreign interference. That, of course, goes for parliamentary elections as well. We hope the interest that produced agreement on the cabinet will prevent a vacancy in the presidency.

Lebanon faces a porous border with Syria that eases terrorist infiltration, Hezbollah's weapon stockpiles that lie beyond government authority and the need to implement U.N. Security Council Resolution 1701 which calls for the disarmament of all armed groups.

Political and sectarian differences have been intensified by the war in Syria. Hezbollah entered that war to protect the Assad regime and to do the bidding of its foreign sponsors. Syrian aircraft and artillery violate Lebanon's borders with impunity.

Lebanese towns near the border, such as Arsal, have borne a particularly heavy burden. A stretched Lebanese Armed Forces has acted to maintain internal security. The LAF has recently undertaken a major operation in Tripoli that has made some progress toward restoring calm and there may be upcoming operations in the Bekaa.

The LAF has the political support to do these operations. The LAF has also had counterterrorism successes last year and this year, capturing high-profile terrorists including a facilitator for al-Qaeda-affiliated groups responsible for a spate of suicide bombings.

My colleague, Deputy Assistant Secretary of Defense Spence, will provide details of our assistance to the LAF. But let me emphasize the importance of the relationships we have formed through our assistance to the LAF and to the Internal Security Forces, as Madam Chairman mentioned.

We seek to increase this assistance in order to build the LAF's capabilities to secure its borders with Syria. Let me also emphasize at the outset that we continually assess our assistance to ensure that no terrorist organizations including Hezbollah influence or benefit from our assistance.

We believe we have an excellent record in this regard. As you know, Saudi Arabia plans to provide $3 billion in aid to the LAF. We are in contact with Saudi Arabia and with France to promote the complementarity that some of you mentioned in order to maximize the growth of the LAF's capabilities.

The Saudi aid in no way obviates the need for continued U.S. assistance which is crucial to meeting needs and building relationships. Deputy Assistant Secretary Spence and I will be travelling to France later this month to engage in continued discussions on just this subject.

Madam Chairman, half of the 1 million Syrian refugees are under the age of 18. The refugees reside in host communities, in rented rooms, unfinished buildings or informal tented settlements throughout the country.

The United States has provided now some $370 million in assistance to help cope with this burden. We urge other countries that have not delivered on their pledges to Lebanon to do so now.

The World Bank estimates that the Syria crisis will have cost Lebanon $7.5 billion by the end of this year and will cut GDP, real GDP growth, by 2.9 percent this year. Reserves of offshore natural gas offer one potential ray of optimism but to date the lengthy political stalemate and the maritime boundary dispute with Israel have prevented further exploration.

We hope the new government will continue efforts to find an arrangement regarding this dispute that will allow the Lebanese people to benefit from these resources.

Madam Chairman, in the face of all of these challenges, U.N. Secretary General Ban Ki-moon and Lebanese President Michel Suleiman mobilized support for Lebanon last September by launching the International Support Group for Lebanon.

This group must be an active vehicle for international support. In 2 days I will join other members of this group and representatives of the LAF to discuss how we can further address Lebanon's security assistance needs.

The United States is also committed to helping end impunity for assassinations and political violence in Lebanon. We strongly support the special tribunal for Lebanon, which has begun trials of those suspected of assassinating former Prime Minister Rafic Hariri and 21 others. The Lebanese people deserve justice.

Chairman Ros-Lehtinen, Ranking Member Deutch, members, Lebanon has had partners to see it through its darkest periods. The Taif Accord helped end the civil war. U.N. Security Council Resolutions 1559 and 1701 helped structure a return to stability.

The Baabda Declaration obligated all Lebanese parties to stay out of regional conflicts. It needs to be implemented by all parties. The United States will remain a partner promoting a stable, secure and sovereign Lebanon free of foreign interference and able to safeguard its interest. That is in our interest.

Thank you very much.

[The prepared statement of Mr. Silverman follows:]

Written Statement
Lawrence R. Silverman
Deputy Assistant Secretary of State for Near Eastern Affairs

House Foreign Affairs Committee
Subcommittee on the Middle East and North Africa
"Lebanon's Security Challenges and U.S. Interests"
April 8, 2014

Chairman Ros-Lehtinen, Ranking Member Deutch, Members of the Subcommittee, thank you for inviting me to testify today on the situation in Lebanon and our policy towards an important country in a very volatile region.

Your hearing comes at a key moment for Lebanon's security and stability – and that of the entire Levant. The massive refugee influx into Lebanon represents an urgent humanitarian crisis. Lebanon hosts the largest refugee population, per capita, in the world. Just five days ago, Lebanon passed the inauspicious milestone of registering its one millionth Syrian refugee, representing over 20 percent of Lebanon's resident population. But the refugee challenge is only one of several that Lebanon's leaders face today. In addition to the refugee crisis, I will discuss today the political, security and economic challenges Lebanon faces, and how the United States is responding to all these challenges, because Lebanon's future affects important U.S. interests in the region.

The United States has a long history of diplomatic engagement with Lebanon to build a partnership that promotes our shared interests in regional stability, the development of democracy, economic prosperity, and the international effort to counter terrorism and violent extremism. We have worked to support and rebuild Lebanese state institutions that were left in ruins as a result of the civil war, and we have provided development assistance that helps to improve the lives and livelihoods of Lebanese citizens. Since the end of Syria's occupation of Lebanon in 2005, we have accelerated our assistance to crucial state institutions to enable them to take on the leadership roles and management functions that a national government should perform. Our goal is to have an effective partner for the long term that shares our concerns and is actively helping stabilize the region.

Madam Chairman, it is essential that the international community stand by responsible forces in Lebanon in a broader sense, and particularly so in the next several months. Let me explain why.

Political Challenges

Lebanon is at a critical point in its attempt to establish lasting stability and an effective political system, but the conflict in Syria threatens the progress that has been made. Lebanon's political leaders face three political hurdles in the first few months of this year. So far, they have passed two of them – forming a cabinet and getting its ministerial statement approved by Parliament, and the Lebanese people expect them to pass the third – the election of a president. The March 20 approval of Prime Minister Salam's cabinet, after months of stalemate, is a welcome development for the Lebanese people and an opportunity for the United States and Lebanon to work together toward shared goals.

We also welcomed the agreement on a ministerial statement – this cabinet's policy platform – that enabled it to obtain a vote of confidence and thus become empowered to address all issues. After nearly one year with a caretaker cabinet that did not have the authority to respond fully to Lebanon's challenges, this was a critical development. In all the focus on the Syrian conflict and its impact on Lebanon, we sometimes forget that the Lebanese government faces all the normal tasks other governments do, including many pending critical decisions affecting the economy. The new government now has the power to address these issues, and we look forward to it doing so.

The Lebanese people deserve a government that responds to their needs and protects their interests. This new government is comprised of eight members from the March 14 coalition, eight from the March 8 coalition, and eight others without formal affiliation. The government is in a sense an improvement over its predecessor: nearly all political factions are represented in a careful balance, and after three years outside of government, the pro-Western March 14 coalition is now part of the cabinet. It is clear that the March 14 coalition determined that its interests in stabilizing Lebanon and promoting democracy and good governance were better served by participating in this government. We look forward to working with the new government; how we will work with it will depend on its policies and its actions.

President Sleiman's term in office is scheduled to end on May 25. We have made clear to all those concerned in Lebanon that the United States strongly believes that presidential elections should be conducted on time, freely and fairly, in keeping with the constitution, and without foreign interference. We hope that the interest in a stable Lebanon that drove the parties to reach agreement on the new cabinet will also drive them to ensure that there is no vacancy in the presidency, the highest position reserved for Christians in the country. To fail to peacefully transfer power to a president could undermine the momentum created by the formation of a fully-empowered government. At this critical moment, Lebanon needs responsible leadership that will address the challenges facing Lebanon and fulfill Lebanon's international obligations.

Security Challenges

Lebanon faces unique and serious security problems: an un-demarcated and porous border with Syria that sees terrorist infiltration in both directions; areas of the country outside full state control; Hizballah's weapon stockpiles that lie beyond government authority; the continuing need to implement UNSCR 1701, which calls for the disarmament of all armed groups in Lebanon and stresses the importance of full control of Lebanon by the government of Lebanon; and a history of foreign interference in Lebanese internal matters.

Challenges to security are rising. Existing political and sectarian differences have been intensified by the war in Syria; Hizballah entered that war against the earlier agreement of all Lebanese parties and the government to "dissociate" the country from foreign conflicts. The Lebanese people know only too well the repercussions of spillover from the Asad regime's brutal suppression of its own people. Syrian aircraft and artillery continue to violate Lebanon's borders with impunity, killing and wounding Lebanese civilians and Syrian refugees alike. Lebanese towns near the border with Syria, such as Arsal, have borne a particularly heavy burden – both of refugees and of violence.

Hizballah is dragging the Lebanese people into a war as it protects and empowers the Asad regime, whose continuation can only result in more conflict, more acts of terror, and more potential instability for Lebanon. Hizballah clearly does so not in the interest of Lebanon, but in its own narrow interests and on behalf of its foreign sponsors. Its participation in the war in Syria has also helped to draw foreign fighters– both Shia and Sunni – to Syria, increasing the risk of radicalized fighters bringing terror back to their home countries. Hizballah's posture of acting inside the state when it is convenient, but stepping outside the state to use arms and violence for its self-interests, remains deeply disturbing and destabilizing. That is why the implementation of UNSCR 1701 is so necessary.

And now, extremists fighting the Asad regime and its Hizballah backers have brought that fight inside Lebanon, through a wave of reprehensible terrorist attacks that have killed and injured scores in Beirut and other cities. The United States has condemned those terrorist attacks. Lebanon needs to be spared this politically and economically damaging cycle of violence begun by Hizballah's interference in an internal struggle in Syria. The United States, the Government of Lebanon, and the Lebanese people share this goal.

In this tough environment, a significantly stretched Lebanese Armed Forces (LAF) has acted to maintain internal security, and it has taken losses in those operations, as has the Internal Security Forces (ISF), both of which receive U.S. assistance. Over 16 LAF soldiers were killed in a June 2013 attempt to arrest an extremist and his followers in Sidon; three were killed by violent extremists on March 29th of this year. The LAF is currently undertaking a major operation in the northern city of Tripoli to help end politico-sectarian clashes and calm tensions. They have made progress in this regard. The security forces are also deploying to the northern and central Bekaa to calm tensions there.

The LAF has had recent counter-terrorism successes. It has captured a number of high-profile terrorists, including a facilitator for several al Qa'ida-affiliated groups that have carried out a spate of brutal suicide bombings in Beirut, Hermel, and other Lebanese towns. We share Lebanon's concerns over the presence and activities of these extremists. This is not just a Lebanese problem; the growth of this extremist presence in Lebanon is a key focus of the United States and our international partners. Within Lebanon, these abhorrent acts of terrorism threaten the principles of stability, freedom, and safety that the people of Lebanon have worked so hard to uphold; they also damage the economy. We urge all parties in Lebanon to refrain from retaliatory acts that contribute to the cycle of violence.

These incidents highlight the ongoing dangers to Lebanon from the conflict in Syria, Hizballah's armed support for the Asad regime, and the flow of violent extremists (including the Nusrah Front, the Islamic State of Iraq and the Levant, and the Abdullah Azzam Brigades) into Lebanon. The states from which these fighters are coming are indeed concerned about the dangers these fighters will present when they return to their home countries. Stopping these flows and the flow of private financing to extremists is a responsibility of all governments in the region and beyond.

Central to any country's stability is a trained and capable security sector that is accountable to the people and the state. The critical support we provide to the LAF and the ISF is intended to build their capacities to thwart violent extremists and criminal organizations and to ensure security throughout the country, including control along its borders. Our assistance to the LAF strengthens its ability to serve as the sole institution entrusted with the defense of Lebanon's sovereignty.

We seek to increase this assistance in order to modernize the LAF, and in particular to provide training and equipment to help defend its borders with Syria. Clearly, the LAF needs to do more to patrol and secure its borders. And clearly, this is not just a military issue, but a political one as well. It is a priority for those of us providing assistance to the LAF to enhance its capabilities, even as we encourage maximum effort and political support to enable the LAF to assert control over Lebanese territory.

The LAF remains above politics and factional interests, as desired by the vast majority of the Lebanese people. It is a badly needed example of cross-confessional integration for the entire country, and it remains one of the most respected national institutions in Lebanon because it reflects the diversity of the country.

Our sustained support is critical to improving the capabilities of the LAF. For example, our International Military and Education Training programs builds lasting professional relationships between the senior ranks of the LAF and the U.S. military, and strengthens the values of civilian leadership and respect for rule of law within the LAF officer corps. My Department of Defense colleague, Deputy Assistant Secretary of Defense Matt Spence, will provide greater detail of our relationship with the LAF, but I want to emphasize the importance of the relationships we have built with the LAF and with the ISF over the years. Supporting the LAF can also strengthen its ability to serve as a model for other Lebanese institutions.

Our assistance has been effective and is welcomed by the Lebanese people. We need to maintain this partnership in support of our own national interests. In addition, the Department's Antiterrorism Assistance (ATA) program has been working with the ISF since 2006 to build its capacity to investigate terrorist incidents, secure borders to stem the flow of arms and terrorists, and professionalize the ISF leadership. Our partnership with the ISF has been fruitful.

Since 2007, the U.S. government has provided basic and specialized training for over 8,000 ISF members. We are helping to increase ISF effectiveness through training in modern policing practices, in order to enable the ISF to better maintain internal security, a key to helping relieve the Lebanese Armed Forces from law enforcement duties. This is especially important now, with the spillover of violence from Syria and resulting increased demands on the LAF.

Let me emphasize that we continually assess our policy of engagement with and assistance to the Government of Lebanon to ensure that no foreign terrorist organizations (including, but not limited to Hizballah) influence or benefit from the assistance we provide to the LAF and the ISF.

We thank Congress for its continued support of State and Defense programs that provide for Lebanon's security and economic development; these programs have only grown more important in light of the Syria conflict.

As you know, Saudi Arabia has committed to provide $3 billion in assistance to the LAF. International assistance to the LAF can help build up the capabilities the LAF needs. The United States believes international donors should complement each other's efforts in order to maximize the growth of needed capabilities for an armed force whose troops are badly stretched across the country. We are in contact with the governments of Saudi Arabia and France regarding this assistance to promote maximum coordination. However, this does not by any means replace or obviate the need for U.S. assistance, which is crucial to providing the training and capacity-building that the LAF needs and solidifying this important officer-to-officer, soldier-to-soldier relationships.

Humanitarian Challenges

Lebanon hosts more refugees from Syria than any other country – both per capita and in absolute terms. Refugees – half of whom are under the age of 18 – reside in host communities, in rented accommodations, unfinished buildings, or in informal tented settlements in more than 1,600 localities throughout the country. There is not a single Lebanese community that has not been affected by the refugee crisis. With refugee arrivals continuing unabated, the sheer volume of need has overwhelmed the ability of the central government and local municipalities to respond to the enormous challenge of providing public services to this large and growing population.

The United States is doing its part, providing more than $340 million in humanitarian assistance since the beginning of the conflict in Syria to support the needs of refugees in Lebanon and, importantly, the communities that host them. Lebanon does not have formal refugee camps for Syrian refugees; almost all live in Lebanese communities, placing enormous strains on basic infrastructure, health and educational systems. It is essential that the international community address the needs of the host communities as well as those of the refugees. For example, last September at the inaugural meeting of the International Support Group for Lebanon, Secretary Kerry announced an additional $30 million in assistance specifically aimed at helping the communities that host these refugees. This commitment is provided in addition to our on-going economic and development assistance programs that have been adjusted to help Lebanon face these specific challenges.

Some of our assistance provides medical interventions to prevent communicable diseases like polio and hepatitis; other programs provide basic immunizations to every child, whether Lebanese, Syrian, or other nationalities, at border crossings and in refugee-hosting communities. Our assistance also helps improve the quality of Lebanon's public school system, which has been inundated by Syrian school-age children. Our programs refurbish and enlarge dilapidated schools to accommodate a larger student body, and we then equip these schools with educational materials and school supplies. Our assistance also provides psycho-social support to some Syrian, Palestinian, and Lebanese children, who have been traumatized by the war, its effects on civilians, and continuous cross-border attacks on Lebanese communities by the Syrian regime.

In its current humanitarian appeal, the UN is seeking $1.7 billion in 2014 to respond to the refugee crisis in Lebanon, on top of the money that the government of Lebanon is already spending on the humanitarian response. The scope of the crisis is an unprecedented challenge for the UN humanitarian agencies and non-governmental organizations; the Lebanese will face this challenge for some time. We appreciate the generosity and hospitality of the Lebanese government and the Lebanese people and understand the gravity of the situation on Lebanon's fragile society and strained infrastructure. The international community must step up to provide robust humanitarian and development assistance to support refugees and host communities in order to bolster Lebanon's stability while meeting urgent humanitarian needs.

Unfortunately, some countries have not yet delivered on their pledges made at the most recent donors' conference in Kuwait in January. We call on them to join us in doing so. The United States is also committed to reducing the burden on Lebanon and other countries in the region by considering more Syrian refugees for resettlement in the United States. UNHCR has announced its intention to refer to all resettlement countries up to 30,000 Syrian refugees in the region for resettlement by the end of 2014, and up to 100,000 by 2016. We expect to play a leading role by considering thousands of these referrals as UNHCR scales up its program.

Economic Challenges

The spillover of the conflict in Syria, including terrorist attacks in Beirut and elsewhere, has weakened Lebanon's tourism sector, investment, and foreign trade – all important components of Lebanon's open economy. Uncertainty has depressed consumption, with wealthy tourists gone and more Lebanese reluctant to spend. Investors are delaying decisions, and Lebanon's crucial land trade routes have been disrupted. This year will likely be the fourth consecutive year of slowing growth for the Lebanese economy. The World Bank has estimated that the crisis will cut real GDP growth in Lebanon by 2.9 percent this year. The Bank estimated that the conflict cost Lebanon $2.5 billion in lost economic activity in 2013 alone, and could push 170,000 Lebanese into poverty.

U.S. economic assistance programs encourage growth in Lebanon by improving the technical expertise of small business owners and their access to financial resources, especially in the agricultural sector. We also encourage the Lebanese government to do more to promote economic reform, including privatization of its moribund public sector industries, which has been stymied due to political gridlock.

Through U.S. development assistance, we are working to improve the quality and delivery of water services across the country. In North Lebanon, an area estimated to be hosting more than 200,000 refugees, we are installing water networks and improving existing pumping stations in underserved villages, to increase water supply and expand the network to new users. In the Bekaa, we are installing chlorination systems and water networks to enhance the quality of water and increase supply.

The United States also provides scholarships for needy Lebanese students to attend the American University of Beirut and the Lebanese American University. These scholarship recipients, who represent all of Lebanon's geographic, religious, and ethnic diversity, are graduates of the Lebanese public school system who have opportunities to attend American-style universities that are among the best in the region. We do this – educating more than 300 students in the last five years – to bring opportunity to talented but economically disadvantaged students and to invest in a brighter future for Lebanon and the region.

Banking is a pillar of the Lebanese economy, and the banking sector, despite all of Lebanon's economic challenges, saw deposits grow significantly in 2013, providing economic stability through its purchases of government debt and funding of private sector activity. Given its importance, it is all the more critical that the banking sector in Lebanon safeguards Lebanon's place in the international financial system by doing all it can to protect itself and correspondent banks in the U.S. and elsewhere from money laundering and terrorist finance. In coordination with the Treasury Department, we closely engage with the Central Bank of Lebanon and with Lebanese banks to ensure that they have vigorous systems to combat these illicit finance threats. We appreciate the cooperation we have received from the Lebanese banking sector to date and look forward to further cooperation.

The most promising economic sector in Lebanon in the medium- to long-term is the hydrocarbons industry. Lebanon may have substantial reserves of offshore natural gas and maybe even oil deposits. However, the lengthy political stalemate of the last caretaker government, as well as an unresolved maritime boundary with Israel, has prevented Lebanon from further exploring its offshore resources. No exploration has taken place, and any potential finds would take a number of years to begin producing, but U.S. companies are interested in this potential new sector.

The United States engages both the Lebanese and Israelis to encourage an arrangement, without prejudice to competing claims over maritime boundaries, whereby international petroleum companies can have the confidence to explore and develop Lebanon's resources. We hope the new government will continue efforts to find such an arrangement, and we hope the Lebanese people will be able to enjoy the benefits of these resources. Deputy Assistant Secretary of State Amos Hochstein has been engaged with Lebanese officials and was in Beirut last week for discussions with the new government. We continue to make progress toward a mutual understanding between Israel and Lebanon and continue to encourage both sides to avoid activity in the disputed area.

The Importance of Broad International Support

In the face of all the challenges I have cited, UN Secretary General Ban Ki-moon and President Michel Sleiman mobilized support for Lebanon's stability, sovereignty, and state institutions by launching last September the International Support Group for Lebanon, which currently consists of the UN, the permanent members of the UN Security Council, the World Bank, the Arab League, Germany, Italy, and the EU. It was a strong demonstration of international support for Lebanon's sovereignty and stability, and for responsible Lebanese political actors. We look to the ISG to be an active vehicle by which the international community can demonstrate political and financial support to promote stability and to help Lebanon address specific challenges. In two days' time, I will join representatives from other ISG member nations in Rome to discuss with representatives from the LAF how the international community can further address Lebanon's security assistance needs in an effective way.

The United States, along with many others in the international community, is committed to ensuring an end to the era of impunity for assassinations and political violence in Lebanon. That is why we strongly support the work of the Special Tribunal for Lebanon. Three months ago, the Tribunal began its initial trials to bring to justice those responsible for assassinating former Prime Minister Rafik Hariri in 2005, along with 21 innocents killed in this and other attacks. The Lebanese people deserve accountability and justice. The commencement of the trials is an important step, but political violence still plagues Lebanon. Last December, former Finance Minister and Ambassador to the United States Mohammad Chatah was assassinated in downtown Beirut – a great loss for Lebanon. Two other March 14 leaders survived assassination attempts in 2012 – a minister in the current cabinet, Boutros Harb, and Lebanese Forces leader Samir Geagea. Respected ISF Information Branch Chief Wissam al-Hassan was killed in a car bomb in Beirut in October 2012. We urge the entire international community to support the Lebanese people's quest for accountability in these cases.

Chairman Ros-Lehtinen, Ranking Member Deutch, Members,

Lebanon has faced many existential challenges since gaining independence in 1943, and today it faces similar challenges from the war in Syria. Lebanon has found reliable international partners to see it through some of its darkest periods and emerge the stronger for it. The 1989 Taif Accord was the basis for ending 15 years of civil war, and its multi-confessional National Pact remains in effect. UN Security Council Resolutions 1559 and 1701 helped structure a return to stability. The 2012 Baabda Declaration established the principle that all Lebanese parties and factions should abstain from regional conflicts; it needs to be implemented by all parties.

But Lebanon also has friends. The United States is one of them, and will remain so. We need to stand with the people of Lebanon – not just to stand for our principles, but to serve our national interests, including the promotion of a stable, secure and sovereign Lebanon, one that is free of foreign interference and that is able to defend its own interests. And we will continue our efforts to end the conflict in Syria; otherwise, that conflict will continue to destabilize Lebanon and other states in the region.

Thank you again for this opportunity. I look forward to your questions.

Ms. Ros-Lehtinen. Thank you, Mr. Silverman. We appreciate it. Dr. Spence.

STATEMENT OF MATTHEW SPENCE, PH.D., DEPUTY ASSISTANT SECRETARY OF DEFENSE FOR MIDDLE EAST POLICY, U.S. DEPARTMENT OF DEFENSE

Mr. Spence. Chairman Ros-Lehtinen, Ranking Member Deutch and other distinguished members of this committee, thank you for the opportunity to speak with you about the security situation in Lebanon, the importance of our partnership with the Lebanese Armed Forces and thank you for your comments calling attention to the critical nature of this issue right now.

The impact of the Syrian conflict on Lebanon is stark. I visited Lebanon in January with the purpose of evaluating first-hand the deteriorating security situation there. I met with President Suleiman, General Kahwagi and other senior Lebanese officials and members of the Lebanese Armed Forces.

It was very clear to me that more than ever United States security cooperation is essential to helping maintain Lebanon's stability. This is essential for America's national interests as well as that of Lebanon and America's allies and partners in the region.

Just last week, as many of you have noted, the United Nations reported there are now more than 1 million refugees in Lebanon from Syria. That is equal to over 20 percent of the population of Lebanon.

It is a figure that rightly gives all of us pause. Now, despite Lebanon's official disassociation policy regarding the Syrian conflict, Hezbollah is militarily and, I would say, nefariously involved in Syria and sectarian tensions are spilling over increasingly over the Syria-Lebanon border.

Lebanese towns and villages near the border with Syria are regularly experiencing shelling from Syria both by the Syrian regime and by Syrian opposition forces and terrorists.

The Syrian conflict is in fact incubating extremism on both sides of the sectarian divide. One of the most concerning aspects of the Syrian conflict from the U.S. security perspective is that it is attracting foreign fighters from across the region and from around the world.

We assess that there are now significantly more foreign fighters in Syria than there were foreign fighters in Iraq at the height of the Iraq war. The Assad regime is receiving active support from Iran and from Hezbollah. This is unacceptable.

Many other foreign fighters are finding their way into a number of fighting units including terrorist groups, the al-Nusra Front and the Islamic State of Iraq and the Levant. These foreign fighters are becoming battle hardened and they are gaining experience that could have destabilizing effects in the years to come.

Both the Islamic State of Iraq and the Levant and al-Nusra Front have established a presence in Lebanon and they are seeking to increase their cooperation with Sunni extremist groups already operating there.

And I would also add that terrorist attacks in Lebanon are on the rise. Since the beginning of 2014 alone, nine suicide attacks have hit Shi'a population centers and Lebanese Armed Forces targets. But those are not the only attacks.

Last year, two Sunni mosques were bombed and a leading Sunni politician and former Ambassador to the United States was assassinated. Leaders from across Lebanon's political spectrum have condemned these attacks rightly so and called for unity and cooperation with the Lebanese Armed Forces.

The Lebanese Armed Forces have taken a variety of bold measures to maintain stability in Lebanon and counter the destabilizing effects that the Syrian conflict risks to Lebanese security. They have taken important steps but, of course, there is more, far more to be done.

In the last 7 months, we have seen our partners and the Lebanese special forces deploy to Sidon for counterterrorism operations, to Tripoli to conduct stability operations and Arsal to provide security for the population affected by Syria's instability.

In fact, in the past few days the Lebanese Armed Forces and the Internal Security Forces of Lebanon have successfully conducted large-scale operations in Tripoli based on the new government's Tripoli security plan that plans to stem the violent sectarian violence in that city.

Now, unfortunately, the LAF's willingness and commitment to exercise its role as the sole legitimate defense force in Lebanon has made it a target as well and just over a week ago we have seen Lebanese armed forces personnel targeted as a result.

Now, in the face of these rising challenges the LAF has demonstrated considerable unity, fortitude and professionalism as evidenced in the recent counterterrorism success. And the counterterrorism fight that Lebanon faces, of course, is not just in Lebanon's interest but in our interest as well.

To fight successfully against terrorism, an army must be well equipped, properly trained and supported by its partners. That is why the United States' role is so important.

As my interaction in Lebanon with a variety of political and military officials has confirmed, strengthening the Lebanese Armed Forces is essential at this time when sectarian tensions are increasing due to the Syrian conflict.

U.S. assistance to the Lebanese Armed Forces has helped strengthen its capacity and support its mission to secure Lebanese borders, defend the sovereignty of the state of Lebanon and implement U.N. Security Council Resolutions 1559 and 1701.

Significantly, strengthening the LAF will help combat Hezbollah by undermining Hezbollah's justification for maintaining its arms as will Hezbollah's false claim to be acting in the interests of the Lebanese people.

In conclusion, Madam Chairman and Ranking Member Deutch, I would say that the challenge of supporting the Lebanese people and the security and stability of the Lebanon state is no more important than it is right now.

The Lebanese Armed Forces is a critical pillar of Lebanon stability and its commitment to curtailing sectarian fighting and terrorism has been a significant factor in preventing Lebanon from descending into greater violence.

Our position is to work closely with you to continue that support. Thank you for the opportunity to speak with you today.

[The prepared statement of Mr. Spence follows:]

23

Written Statement
Matthew J. Spence
Deputy Assistant Secretary of Defense, Middle East Policy
U.S. Department of Defense

House Foreign Affairs Committee
Subcommittee on the Middle East and North Africa
"Lebanon's Security Challenges and U.S. Interests"
April 8, 2014

Chairman Ros-Lehtinen, Ranking Member Deutch, and other distinguished Members of the Subcommittee, thank you for the opportunity to speak to you today about the evolving security situation in Lebanon and the importance of our partnership with the Lebanese Armed Forces (LAF).

The impact of the Syrian conflict on Lebanon is stark. I visited Lebanon in January to discuss the deteriorating security situation with Lebanese officials and members of the Lebanese Armed Forces, and it is clear to me now, more than ever, that U.S. security cooperation is essential to helping to maintain Lebanon's stability. As reported by the UN last week, there are now more than one million refugees in Lebanon from Syria, equal to approximately 20 percent of the current population in Lebanon. Despite Lebanon's official disassociation policy regarding the Syrian conflict, Hizballah is militarily involved in Syria, and sectarian tensions are increasingly spilling over the Syria-Lebanon border. Lebanese towns and villages near the border with Syria regularly experience shelling from Syria – both by the Syrian regime and Syrian opposition forces and terrorists – due to regime allegations that opposition fighters use Sunni-dominated areas as safe havens, as well as opposition retaliation against Hizballah for fighting on behalf of the Syrian regime.

24

The Syrian conflict is an incubator of extremism – on both sides of the sectarian divide. One of the most concerning aspects of the Syrian conflict from a U.S. security perspective is that it is attracting foreign fighters from across the region and around the world. We assess that there are now significantly more foreign fighters in Syria than there were foreign fighters in Iraq at the height of the Iraq war. The Asad regime is receiving active support from Iran and Hizballah. Many other fighters are finding their way to a variety of fighting units, including terrorist groups such as the al Nusrah Front, and the Islamic State of Iraq and the Levant. These foreign fighters are becoming battle-hardened and gaining experience that could have destabilizing effects in the years to come. The Islamic State of Iraq and the Levant, in particular, has exploited the governing vacuum in eastern Syria to carve out territory to train its fighters, recruit more of them, and plan attacks. Both the Islamic State of Iraq and the Levant and al Nusrah Front have established a presence in Lebanon and are seeking to increase their cooperation with Sunni violent extremist groups already operating there. These Lebanon-based groups have claimed a number of recent suicide attacks in Lebanon.

Sunni terrorist attacks in Lebanon are on the rise. Since the beginning of 2014 alone, nine suicide attacks have hit Shia population centers and LAF targets. But those are not the only attacks. Last year two Sunni mosques in Lebanon's second biggest city, Tripoli, were targeted by car bombs and a leading Sunni politician and former Ambassador to the United States, Mohammad Chatah, was assassinated in Beirut. Leaders from across Lebanon's political spectrum have condemned these attacks and have called for unity and cooperation with the Lebanese Armed Forces.

The Lebanese Armed Forces and Stability

The Lebanese Armed Forces have taken a variety of bold measures to maintain stability in Lebanon and counter the destabilizing effects that the Syrian conflict risks to Lebanon's security. The increased operational tempo of Lebanese Armed Forces deployments over the past few months reflects the LAF's commitment to Lebanon's security. In the last seven months, we have seen our partners in the Lebanese Special Forces deploy to Sidon for counterterrorism operations, to Tripoli to conduct stability operations, and to Arsal to provide security for the populations affected by Syria's instability. In the past few days, the LAF and Internal Security Forces (ISF) have successfully conducted large-scale operations in Tripoli based on the new government's Tripoli security plan to stem the spiraling sectarian violence in the city. Throughout this period, the 2nd Intervention Regiment conducted stability operations and supported counterterrorism and counternarcotics efforts in the Bekaa Valley.

The LAF's willingness and commitment to exercise its role as the sole legitimate defense force in Lebanon has made it a target as well. Just over a week ago, three Lebanese Armed Forces personnel were killed when a suicide bomber detonated his vehicle at an LAF checkpoint on the outskirts of Arsal, a city near the border with Syria.

In the face of these rising challenges, the LAF has demonstrated considerable unity, fortitude, and professionalism. The Lebanese Armed Forces have organized themselves effectively to maintain a tremendously high operational tempo for many of its units, and have demonstrated the ability to make appropriate requests for and use of equipment, as well as unity and professionalism in numerous operations. The LAF's professionalism and commitment are evident in their multiple counter-terrorism successes. As reported in the press, the LAF has disrupted several terrorist plots in recent weeks. In February, the Lebanese Armed Forces arrested a terrorist attack facilitator, which led to the discovery and dismantling of multiple car bombs and the disruption of on-going attack plans. On March 27, the LAF conducted an operation that removed a key bomb-maker for al Nusra Front in the Sunni stronghold of Arsal. These operations have not been without their costs; seven LAF soldiers have been killed in Sunni terrorist attacks targeting the LAF since last summer. However, to fight successfully and win against terrorism, an army must be properly equipped, trained, and supported by its partners.

U.S. Support to the Lebanese Armed Forces

As my interactions in Lebanon with a variety of political and military actors confirmed, our continued engagement and assistance to the Lebanese Armed Forces are all the more important in this time of increased challenges to Lebanon's stability. U.S. and international assistance builds the capacity of the Lebanese Armed Forces to serve the democratic government and people of Lebanon. The Lebanese Armed Forces are an effective, non-sectarian institution with widespread national support, which is essential at a time when the sectarian tensions in Lebanon are increasing due to the Syrian conflict.

Supporting the Lebanese Armed Forces as Lebanon's sole legitimate defense force is a critical component of Lebanon's long-term stability and development. Strengthening the LAF will help undermine Hizballah's justification for maintaining its arms as well as its claim to be acting in defense of Lebanon's interests. Our assistance has also enabled the LAF to combat al-Qaeda-affiliated terrorists seeking to establish a foothold in Lebanon.

U.S. assistance to the Lebanese Armed Forces -- approximately $71 million in fiscal year 2013 Foreign Military Financing (FMF) funds – helps strengthen the capacity of the Lebanese Armed Forces and support its mission to secure Lebanon's borders, defend the sovereignty of the State, and implement UN Security Council Resolutions 1559 and 1701. Since FY 2006, the

United States has allocated more than $1 billion in security assistance to support the Lebanese Armed Forces and Internal Security Forces. U.S. security cooperation is a key pillar of our bilateral relationship.

In December 2013, President Sleiman announced that Saudi Arabia will grant Lebanon $3 billion to purchase defense equipment from the French. In concert with international partners such as the French and Saudis, and in line with the International Support Group for Lebanon, we fully support strengthening the Lebanese Armed Forces and will continue to work with partners to ensure that U.S. assistance is complementary and used effectively to meet these growing challenges. In line with this, I am traveling to France later this month to discuss our mutual efforts and complementary assistance in Lebanon.

Our International Military Education and Training (IMET) program with Lebanon is the fourth largest IMET program in the world. IMET builds strong ties between the United States and Lebanon by bringing Lebanese officers and officials to the United States for professional development and to train alongside U.S. forces. For example, in fiscal year 2013, the IMET program supported 68 Lebanese military students to attend education and training classes in the United States. Since 1985, the IMET program has brought more than 1,000 Lebanese military students to the United States for education and training.

Our Section 1206 assistance has enhanced the Lebanese Armed Forces' ability to monitor, secure, and protect Lebanon's borders against terrorist threats and the illicit transfer of goods. Most recently, the United States increased funding to enhance Lebanon's border security capability further by providing the Lebanese Armed Forces' 2nd Border Regiment with additional surveillance equipment to guard its portion of the border - including radars, seismic sensors, and cameras.

We are also focused on supporting the Lebanese Armed Forces' desire for institutional reform; the Department of Defense has just started a Defense Institution Reform Initiative (DIRI) with the Lebanese Armed Forces. This initiative complements a U.S. whole-of-government effort supporting Lebanese security sector reform. U.S. Central Command continues to provide support to the training and professionalization of the Lebanese Armed Forces, while the Department of State's Bureau of International Narcotics and Law Enforcement Affairs and Bureau of Counterterrorism jointly fund a program to strengthen the capability and border management capacity of the Internal Security Forces. All of these programs help to strengthen our relationship and ties between our two militaries and throughout their ranks.

As mentioned in Deputy Assistant Secretary of State Larry Silverman's testimony, the Lebanese have agreed upon a new government formed by Prime Minister Tammam Salam. This is an important step for the government and people of Lebanon as the cabinet is able to provide political support to back the LAF's critical work to maintain stability. Having a new cabinet also provides us with an opportunity to increase our engagement with Lebanon's government and the Lebanese Armed Forces in particular.

Supporting Lebanon

Even if the crisis in Syria were to end quickly, the security and economic implications for neighboring Lebanon will be felt for years to come. Our positive relationship with, and continued support to, Lebanon and the Lebanese Armed Forces are now more important than ever. The Lebanese Armed Forces is a critical pillar of Lebanon's stability, and its commitment to curtailing sectarian fighting and terrorism has been a significant factor in preventing Lebanon from descending into greater violence.

UNCLASSIFIED

Representative Ros-Lehtinen and Representative Deutch, I thank you and the other distinguished Members of the Subcommittee for calling this hearing and drawing attention to Lebanon's security challenges and the U.S. security interest in supporting Lebanon during this critical time.

————

Ms. Ros-Lehtinen. Thank you to both gentlemen for excellent testimony. We will begin our question and answer period.

U.S. security cooperation is essential to helping Lebanon maintain stability or at least to help fend off a second civil war.

From Fiscal Year 2009 to 2013, the U.S. allocated nearly $¾ billion for the Lebanese security forces. I recognize the need to send assistance to the LAF and ISF in order to support a stable and secure Lebanon and in order to protect our U.S. national security interests.

However, I also recognize that this is an outrageously high amount of money, equipment and training to dedicate to a Lebanon that has never really been stable nor free from the influence of outside actors.

I commissioned a GAO report on U.S. security assistance to Lebanon which was released in two phases, as you know. GAO found that both State and DoD were deficient in their assessments in evaluating the effectiveness of our security assistance to Lebanon and also deficient in their monitoring of the security equipment transferred to the LAF and ISF.

Both State and DoD concurred with the GAO's findings and recommendations. And so I ask what steps have both agencies taken to ensure that these deficiencies and gaps have been properly addressed in order to maximize the effectiveness of our security assistance to Lebanon and why were these steps not implemented from the beginning? And I will continue.

Mr. Silverman, you mentioned the emergence of a possible hydrocarbon industry for Lebanon in your testimony. However, as you mentioned, there is this unresolved maritime border dispute between Lebanon and Israel which has prevented exploration, delaying any potential investment, and the uncertainty over the future of the Lebanese Government and the instability by all the sectarian violence also play major roles in this.

The administration has been desperately trying to convince Lebanon not to drill in disputed waters until this boundary dispute is resolved, as you mentioned. Can you discuss some of the options we are presenting to try to resolve this dispute and to prevent Lebanon from drilling before a resolution is found?

And on the elections, preparations are under way for a contentious Presidential election. The atmosphere is charged. It could potentially be delayed due to sectarian struggles, and last week as we know the Lebanese forces leader formally announced his candidacy.

What are we doing to help Lebanon ensure that these elections will truly be free and fair and transparent, and what are the probability that these elections will be held on time when Hezbollah could be a major factor in all of this?

And finally, secret talks with Hezbollah—it has been reported late last year that the administration is in secret talks with Hezbollah with the U.K. acting as intermediary. Reports suggest that the administration was willing to warm up to a direct relationship in the future but we have to remember this is a U.S.-designated foreign terrorist organization that is supported by the world's foremost state sponsor of terrorism, Iran, and continues to actively carry out terror attacks against our ally, Israel.

Are these talks going on still and is the administration viewing a warming of relations with Hezbollah as having a possible positive outcome, incredibly enough? And I will refer to you.

Mr. SILVERMAN. Thank you, Madam Chairman. I will deal with the last couple of questions and then we will both deal with the question regarding the GAO report.

First of all, on your last question about our talks continuing, they can't continue because they never existed. Let me say that categorically. It is totally false and we made that clear at the time and not only is it something we are not doing, it is not something that we would do for many of the reasons that you cited.

You didn't mention as well we have had terrorist incidents like the Burgas bombing, you know, in Bulgaria and testimony that came out during the trial in Cyprus, which was clear, again, about Hezbollah's role in terrorism. So let me be absolutely categorical on that point.

Regarding the Presidential elections, we certainly hope that they will not be delayed. We are making our views absolutely clear and I believe that Lebanon is a place that values the opinion of the United States Government and the administration.

These elections need to take place on time, according to the constitution and without foreign interference, and I believe strongly that that is exactly what the Lebanese people want. The Lebanese people, frankly, I think were skeptical that a government could be formed and then it was, and then after that they said but you will never have a ministerial statement and a vote of confidence but then we did have it and it was done——

Ms. ROS-LEHTINEN. Let us get to the GAO because I know our time is limited. Thank you.

Mr. SILVERMAN. Okay. Good. Can I just say one thing about the maritime——

Ms. ROS-LEHTINEN. Sure.

Mr. SILVERMAN [continuing]. The maritime position? Sorry. We are actively working and we had an official there last week to try to encourage that kind of arrangement between Lebanon and Israel to find that arrangement which is mutually acceptable.

So otherwise companies find it difficult. They need a kind of certainty to make an investment in Lebanon. So Lebanon is the one that loses out by not moving—being able to move forward with this legislation. So let me turn to Deputy Assistant Secretary Spence.

Ms. ROS-LEHTINEN. Thank you.

Mr. SPENCE. Sure. Thank you. I would say we are very focused on the issues raised in this report. We are committed to reducing the destabilizing role of Hezbollah and Iran, so thank you for raising the issues in this report.

On the specific question you have, end use monitoring is a critical part of that effort. The report, as you know, Chairman, highlighted that although the Office of Defense Coooperation Beirut had entered some of the end use monitoring information into the computer database, they had not kept physical security checklists for the required 5 years. That needed to be changed. It has been changed and we continue to look at the recommendations to the report carefully.

I would also note that the report helpfully raised that the Lebanese Armed Forces have an excellent track record with end use monitoring. So, again, this is an important issue that we follow. It is critical to countering Hezbollah and we continue to have this as an ongoing process to follow.

Ms. ROS-LEHTINEN. Thank you, and I am way out of time so maybe we will get to the other parts later. Mr. Deutch is recognized.

Mr. DEUTCH. Thank you, Madam Chairman. Deputy Assistant Secretary Silverman, has the flare-up in violence directly related to Hezbollah's involvement in Syria eroded support for Hezbollah in the Shi'ite community and is there any space for an alternative to Hezbollah?

Mr. SILVERMAN. Thank you, Congressman. I think that Hezbollah has been criticized and taken criticism for its involvement in Syria. This is literally the dragging of a people into a war that they did not want and I really think that is reflected in public attitudes toward Hezbollah.

And then, of course, there have been the casualties that Hezbollah has taken. So I think when you see what has happened in Tripoli over the last few days after—between 20 and 30 killed that—and I am hoping you are seeing it, a kind of a rising of a greater consensus both among political leaders and among—certainly among the population that Hezbollah has brought this strike-counterstrike because of their—they initiated the involvement in Syria and people do not want the violence, which has cost them dearly economically.

And so I think there is a real view that enough is enough and that has caused a greater political consensus why we have a government, why we have a ministerial statement that is different and less favorable toward Hezbollah.

Mr. DEUTCH. So how can the United States and the international community strengthen non-Hezbollah factions like the March 14th movement ahead of elections?

Mr. SILVERMAN. I think that is essential. We need to strengthen the institutions. I mentioned the international support group and President—which helped President Suleiman in that critical period very late last year, and our ongoing support for moderate voices in Lebanon and to continue our economic assistance, which is very important.

If we can help them reach this agreement on petroleum—potential petroleum resources that can be a huge boon in coming years and helping them deal with the burden because let me emphasize the burden of the refugees. We always talk about refugees.

We need to talk more about the host communities that are affected by the refugees and some of our aid is going to that. So I think in many ways we are trying to build up what we consider the responsible voices and I think calling for on-time elections according to the constitution help that. Thank you.

Mr. DEUTCH. Thank you. Dr. Spence, some reports indicate that Lebanese Armed Forces are losing the perception of neutrality due to seemingly greater focus on cracking down on Sunni extremists over Hezbollah-affiliated militias. Is that a trend you are seeing?

Mr. SPENCE. You know, one thing that we are most concerned about is making sure the Lebanese Armed Forces can remain a multi sectarian impartial defender of the legitimate use of force for the Lebanese people.

You know, we have seen the Lebanese Armed Forces deploying more on the border and it has been extremist and has often been Sunni extremists which have been moving more. So that is for two reasons.

That is mostly because it has been Sunni extremists have been moving more across the border and right now Hezbollah is actually able to freely pass through the border legally right now.

Mr. DEUTCH. And has—make that last point again.

Mr. SPENCE. So right now the Sunni extremists are the ones who are crossing illegally so it is there. As more border checkpoints have been turned over to the LAF that is what they are doing. Hezbollah is able to pass freely over the border.

Mr. DEUTCH. Well, has U.S. training on border control affected the ability of Iran to smuggle weapons to Hezbollah in any way then?

Mr. SPENCE. It is—you know, it is difficult. I think one thing that we tried to do through our 1206 funding is to provide greater border security and that is everything from monitoring issues across the border. It is allowing the Lebanese Armed Forces to take control of additional border checkpoints that were in control of others before.

That is also setting up new checkpoints. So the border between Lebanon and Syria is one of the most difficult issues we face. But I think that is a key thing that we actually have been able to strengthen the LAF's ability to strengthen the border along the way.

Mr. DEUTCH. Thank you. And finally, Mr. Silverman, you have got 30 seconds left. Just make the case for greater American attention paid to Lebanon. We have, as you know, a hard enough time rallying support and the attention of the American people for any number of crises. Tell us why Lebanon is so important.

Mr. SILVERMAN. Thank you, Congressman. Assistance to Lebanon and maintaining the stability and sovereignty of Lebanon is really critical to our interests in the region.

We need to in effect kind of try to do our best to wall off both Lebanon and other neighbors, and I am talking here about Jordan in particular as well, from the Syrian conflict. We need to show that moderate voices have a place and can run a country and, you know, we don't often—unfortunately, we only talk about Lebanon as an adjunct to the Syria crisis and the war.

That should not be. Lebanon is a normal country trying to do its best and needs to be supported—this is what the Lebanese people want, I believe. This is not an extremist population. We should not abandon this population to whether—throughout the region.

I would say even that the Syrian population is not an extremist population and they shouldn't be abandoned either. So I think it is critical that our assistance is building up the only national institution right now that exists in the wake of this civil war. It comes from a very low baseline, which is why maybe the figures are so high. But I think there is a huge investment and a huge value to maintaining stability and sovereignty in Lebanon. Thank you.

Ms. ROS-LEHTINEN. Thank you, Mr. Deutch. And we will turn to Chairman Steve Chabot of Ohio.

Mr. CHABOT. Thank you very much, Madam Chairman, and thank you for calling this important hearing this morning. It really couldn't come at a more critical time as Lebanon's security continues to be challenged by forces both within and outside its borders.

Hezbollah, of course, continues to be the biggest threat to peace and security in the region. As Lebanon gears up for a Presidential election next month and parliamentary elections in the fall, Hezbollah can be counted on once again to disrupt, intimidate and coerce as it attempts to circumvent the will of the Lebanese people.

Mr. Silverman, let me first of all begin with you. What is the Obama administration doing in its talks with Tehran to stop the Iranian trafficking of weapons to Hezbollah and what kind of discussions are you having with the present Government of Lebanon about it providing cover and protection to Hezbollah?

Mr. SILVERMAN. Thank you, Congressman. Let me make one point first, which is that we understand—all of us understand that this is not a perfect situation in Lebanon. What we worry about and why we focus on the value of this assistance is what would be if we were not providing this assistance, if we left the field to others, let me just—let me just say that.

You know, the talks with Iran that are going on in Vienna right now are focused exclusively on the nuclear issue. Our policy regarding Iran and the actions that we take against Iran's destabilizing policies in the region, destabilizing actions in the region, remain the same, as does our entire sanctions structure against that.

It is absolutely essential that we stand by our allies in the region. That is one of the ways to deal with Iran is by building up our allies in the region.

Mr. CHABOT. Excuse me. Let me just stop you. That is very nice but please answer the question. What are you saying to Iran about them—weapons into Hezbollah? That is the question.

Mr. SILVERMAN. Well, our policy has been clear throughout that we oppose and reject and are calling for an end to——

Mr. CHABOT. Are you saying that to Iran?

Mr. SILVERMAN. Yes, they have.

Mr. CHABOT. You are discussing in those discussions with Iran the weapons going to Lebanon and don't do it?

Mr. SILVERMAN. We have made our—Congressman, we have made our views very clear.

Mr. CHABOT. Is part of those policies——

Mr. SILVERMAN. But the talks in Vienna are focused on the nuclear issue. But we have never stayed away——

Mr. CHABOT. So you are not saying anything about that in those talks?

Mr. SILVERMAN. Those talks are for the nuclear issue.

Mr. CHABOT. Okay. Let me move on. Dr. Spence, what is the LAF, which I believe we have given something like $1 billion of U.S. aid to, what are they doing to curtail Hezbollah's power?

Mr. SPENCE. I think one of the—one of the most important things the Lebanese Armed Forces does to curtail Hezbollah's power is to become the sole legitimate force to provide for the security and stability of Lebanon, and what that does, importantly, is that counters Hezbollah's narrative that only Hezbollah can provide for the use of force and the protection of security of the Lebanese people.

So the more that we can strengthen the LAF it takes away one of Hezbollah's best arguments which we think is a wrong argument—that they are the ones defending the Lebanese—the Lebanese people.

Mr. CHABOT. Okay. What is the administration currently doing in diplomatic discussions with our international partners about Hezbollah's international financial presence and the seeming tolerance of Hezbollah by allies—our allies like France and U.K. and the E.U. in general, despite the E.U.'s terrorist labeling of Hezbollah's military wing?

And also, because I have only got about a minute to go, do you see any prospects for Hezbollah an alternative within the Shi'a community in Lebanon? And I know that is probably a tall order when Hezbollah gets so much of its funding and weapons from outside sources like Iran.

Mr. SILVERMAN. Congressman, on your first point, we have been advocating for a long time that our European colleagues join us in our—in sanctions and measures taken against Hezbollah's financial networks.

And finally, last year they took this, as you say, this designation of the military wing. Let me make clear we don't distinguish between political and military wings of Hezbollah. For us they don't exist.

They should have designated Hezbollah full stop but they took this step and I will tell you, because I have been involved in it and others, it is a constant effort to push for actual implementation. We are—kind of interior structures are dealing with the Europeans constantly to make that designation effective.

I will just tell you one thing that literally just today Germany banned a group that it considers raising money for Hezbollah. That is a positive step. I hope it will be echoed by others. I think there is much more that can be done on this score and we have to do it.

With respect to your second question, Congressman, there are other—Hezbollah does not represent all Shi'a—Lebanese Shi'a. There are other politicians. There are other political groups that represent the Shi'a.

Like I said, I believe that there can be a greater consensus, a broader consensus among the Lebanese people that will build up that reject what Hezbollah has done in dragging them into a war which they never wanted.

Mr. CHABOT. Thank you. My time has expired.

Ms. ROS-LEHTINEN. Thank you very much. Excellent questions, Mr. Chabot. And we will turn now to Mr. Schneider of Illinois.

Mr. SCHNEIDER. Thank you very much and again thank you for your testimony. Mr. Silverman, in your response to one of the earlier questions you mentioned that Lebanon is a normal country trying to do its best, and I might take issue it is a normal country. I see Lebanon more as a delicate balance of an ethnic jigsaw that has been for a long time trying to maintain that semblance of balance.

My question specifically is with the inflow of over 1 million refugees from Syria—what is happening to that balance? What is happening from an economic standpoint, from a demographic but more importantly from a sectarian standpoint?

Mr. SILVERMAN. First of all, Congressman, thank you. I mean, that is right. Lebanon is not in a normal situation. I take the point. What I wanted to stress was it has many normal issues that any government has to do.

For example, it needs to pass two pieces of legislation, two decrees, or else you will not see the exploration of these petroleum resources. The previous government couldn't do it because it wasn't empowered.

This government is empowered. That is one of the things it has to do. It is also facing the civil servants' effort to raise wages. So they do deal with the normal thing.

Clearly, Hezbollah's dragging of Lebanon into this war has raised sectarian divides and tensions and now that is what has to be ratcheted back. That is why having this real government that almost across the entire spectrum is so important and that is why we feel that the political leaders must build upon the two steps that they have taken by electing a President and then carrying out the parliamentary elections.

That, in the end, is the best way of getting at the sectarianism because it is a minority. There are sects but they are a minority that—a small minority that promote sectarian tension. This is what we saw in Tripoli. When the LAF came in people welcomed it—please calm what is going on here and you see this in Arsal.

So we believe very strongly there is the nucleus, the great majority nucleus, that don't want any further sectarian divide. It is having an incredibly damaging effect. Tourism, for example—a lot of tourism from the Gulf. No, not under these circumstances of the violence. So it is very practical for the Lebanese. The losses that Congressman Deutch cited, for example, are huge.

Mr. SCHNEIDER. Right. So as you see, as you said, 1 million refugees have come in. There is no prospect at least on the horizon for a settlement in Syria so they are likely to be in Lebanon for a long time. What implication does that have? What policy should the United States be pursuing to make sure that doesn't lead Lebanon into further sectarian strife?

Mr. SILVERMAN. I think one thing is if we, and it can't just be the United States, as generous as we have been. We have been the number-one donor, $1.7 billion total for the Syrian conflict both in Syria—inside Syria and the region.

The international community has to step up to deal with the effects of the refugee population so that host communities are not feeling—not receiving fewer health services, less water provision, schools, health clinics, all of these things because when the host communities feel this that is potential—that is a potential seed bed, you know, that can increase sectarian tension.

And that is, I think, the best way to get at it, is to try to accommodate the Syrian refugees for as long as they are there and the Lebanese people and the Lebanese Government have been very generous in this regard. But the international community has to step up and try to manage this. That is all it is managing.

Mr. SCHNEIDER. Okay. And with my minute left, let me turn to Dr. Spence because that sectarian balance also has been historically reflected in the makeup of the LAF and with so many new refugees coming in, with the Hezbollah fighters now in Syria that balance kind of is getting rejiggered. What impact and what is being done to make sure that that doesn't lead to sectarian fighting within the LAF?

Mr. SPENCE. I think—I think, look, you rightly point out one of the concerns we have for changing the overall population demographics of Lebanon and I think as you noted it is something that stretches across all the different areas of this.

We try to do it in a few ways. We think our engagement and training with the Lebanese Armed Forces does help reinforce the military professionalism about the idea of working with people who came from very different backgrounds or there may be sectarian fighting outside of the army.

That is one of the reasons why we have the IMET program. The IMET program does help do real training, which isn't just one off but it is getting an understanding how do units deal with the difficulties when different people come together. It is the fourth largest we have in the world.

That is—we have ongoing training programs within Lebanon and it is also an issue that we follow very closely because if we do see issues like that as we illustrated or as you mentioned it will be very, very detrimental to the project we are trying to achieve.

Mr. SILVERMAN. May I just add something, Congressman?

Mr. SCHNEIDER. With permission.

Ms. ROS-LEHTINEN. Absolutely. Without objection.

Mr. SCHNEIDER. Thank you.

Mr. SILVERMAN. Sorry. I just wanted to add that this goes also for our assistance and our training of the Internal Security Forces. They are, along with the LAF, sometimes responsible for dealing with the aftermath of bombings of people, assassination attempts, and for them to be able to do a more professional job that allows for greater accountability can build the confidence of the population. They need that accountability for such acts. Thank you.

Mr. SCHNEIDER. Thank you. I yield back my time.

Ms. ROS-LEHTINEN. Thank you, Mr. Schneider. Mr. Kinzinger of Illinois.

Mr. KINZINGER. Thank you, Madame Chair, and thank you both for being here. Thanks for your service and we appreciate your time.

A couple of points I want to hit but first I want to make some comments. I think the thing that is getting somewhat—well, not really getting lost but that deserves some more discussion is the role that the Syrian conflict is playing in everything right now.

I believe that it was a dire mistake of the United States to fail to enforce the red line that the President put out. I believe that that further reinforced a perception that I think is pretty close to reality—that America is retreating from the Middle East, that America no longer has an interest in what occurs in the Middle

East, and I think this does nothing but embolden our enemies and enemies of our way of life and enemies of freedom.

I would like to remind everybody that there are about 160,000 dead innocent Syrians as a result of Assad's brutal dictatorship. He has gone from using chemical weapons, though he has not destroyed them as he has promised—he has gone from using chemical weapons to now using an almost equally terrifying thing called a barrel bomb where you pack a 55-gallon-drum full of explosives and igniter fluid and drop it on an innocent population and clear a block simply because you don't want people present in a certain geographic location and who cares who dies in the process.

So I think it is very important that as we discuss this we remember the brutality that is occurring and I would encourage the administration to get involved in what is going on in Syria in a much bigger way—arming the moderate rebels, bringing down the rebels that we don't agree with that are linked to al-Qaeda and other extremist organizations.

The one thing I would like to say too, and I guess I will ask this in the form of a question, in terms of the refugee crisis in Lebanon, how is this destabilizing Lebanon? What is the United States doing to try to mitigate some of the problems that are coming along with that and also are you seeing bad actors coming over the border simply pretending to be refugees when in fact they seek to destabilize Lebanon?

Mr. SILVERMAN. Congressman, thank you very much. On the last question, this is a constant concern both for us and for the host governments and, again, it is not Lebanon only. Jordan, for example, faces the same and Turkey faces the same problem.

So it is of concern. You may in any event, and it is something that we are coordinating with our neighbors very closely on to try to stop. And let me say, and this gets to the remarks that you made earlier, we have sharply increased our coordination with our allies who are also assisting the moderate opposition and also coordinating more with our allies on preventing support to extremists and preventing the flow of extremists into Syria.

Is it satisfactory? Absolutely not, and nobody can be satisfied with the situation, which is incredibly brutal. I lived in Syria under the previous Assad but we all know how absolutely brutal this regime is.

So there is that effort to get at not only the flow of extremists but also the financing of extremists.

Mr. KINZINGER. I appreciate that and back to the Syria thing a bit, I hope that—I mean, I hear from administration officials that we are doing such a wonderful job in Syria, which, I mean, and I understand your position. This is not against you but I am not buying it and, you know, frankly, when all our Middle East allies tell us that we are doing absolutely nothing, I think it is pretty obvious that as people continue to go through the meat grinder of innocent folks being killed the United States is standing by when I think there is a lot more we can do.

Let us talk about the situation of the Christian community in Lebanon. I think this is something that when we talk about the Sunni-Shi'a conflict sometimes it gets lost. Can you talk to the situation of the Christians in Lebanon, sir?

Mr. SILVERMAN. Thank you, Congressman. Yes. I mean, Lebanon has a uniquely active and influential and political population in Lebanon which has a unique role in the presidency, in the leadership of the LAF.

Let me just say that, though, that does not mean, for example, that all Christians are united in any particular position including about Presidential candidates, as you know. So the——

Mr. KINZINGER. They are not here either so——

Mr. SILVERMAN. But the Christian community is absolutely vital to Lebanon's future and it is, thanks to various agreements over the years built into the system, the role—the important role that they have and, of course, we are very supportive of that role.

Mr. KINZINGER. Thank you, and thank you again for you all being here and your service and, Madam Chair, thank you for holding the hearing and I yield back.

Ms. ROS-LEHTINEN. Thank you, sir. Mr. Higgins of New York.

Mr. HIGGINS. Thank you, Madam Chair. I think, you know, when we are dealing with Lebanon, you know, again, I think we are dealing with a microcosm of the Middle East, which is, you know, highly pluralistic.

In Lebanon you have 17 different religious sects. You have over 50 percent Muslim population. The population in the Muslim community is almost evenly split between Sunni and Shi'a. About 40 percent of the population is Christian in a nation of less than 6 million people, with Lebanese Sunni jihadis and Shi'a militia Hezbollah.

You know, the national armed forces has been viewed as highly integrated and serving as a buffer between warring factions and it was viewed historically as highly functional as well. And some would argue that the Lebanese Armed Forces are the only true national organization. Now they are in the crossfire in a battle between Shi'a and Sunni.

I think the mistake that we make here in this committee and as a nation is that we view, you know, the situation in Syria as, you know, a bad guy, Bashar al-Assad, who clearly is. You know, he kills 100,000 or more of his people through chemical weapons. But on the other side, you have got al-Qaeda affiliates. You have got Islamic extremists who are the best fighters.

So we have these false choices here as though, you know, because Bashar al-Assad kills 130,000 people through chemical weapons the other side beheads people. You know, so pick your choice of demise, I guess.

And I think the people unfortunately that are true in their democratic aspirations for these countries, be it in Lebanon, be it in Syria, be it in Egypt, they are the vast minority and they don't know how to achieve military success because they truly want, I think, freedom and democracy. But they are not the majority of the people.

And the people who are taking up all the space in these countries are the people who are fighters, not for freedom and democracy but for power. Why do people continue to support Bashar al-Assad who is a Alawite, which is about 7 percent of the Syrian population, because if you are a minority you fear that if the Sunni majority takes over you are going to get slaughtered.

So, you know, these are issues that, you know, there are not all these binary choices. We have got a lot of complexity, a lot of nuance, a lot of gray area that we have to deal with.

I will just give you another example. In Iraq, I can remember traveling there and meeting with Nouri al-Maliki, and Nouri al-Maliki dismissed the congressional delegation's concerns that there wasn't enough being done by his government, a Shi'a, the majority in the country, to embrace the Sunni community.

So he dismisses it by saying, I have other allies in the region, and at that time what he was referring to was Ahmadinejad, his Shi'a ally in Iran. Well, guess who was at the White House a couple of months ago seeking help from the United States to deal with al-Qaeda, who has reemerged as a major influence in Fallujah? Nouri al-Maliki.

We are getting played all over that region and unless and until that region realizes that they are a pluralistic society, until they guarantee rights for minorities, these issues will never be resolved. Your thoughts?

Mr. SILVERMAN. Thank you, Congressman. I will say that we firmly believe that the majority of the population of Syria are not extremists. They are the loud—they are making a lot of noise. They are brutal, absolutely.

You know, our Syria strategy is not just countering and trying to bring about a political transition in Syria. It is also about countering violent extremism, absolutely, and to prevent the terrorists safe haven.

I will say that the Assad regime has manipulated this issue. I mean, the policies of the Assad regime have acted as a magnet for extremists to come to Syria. Then in reaction to that or dealing it tries to draw a benefit from that by presenting not just minorities but all Syrians with a choice.

It is either us or those extremists, and that is a false choice too because what they are doing is actually attracting extremism and strengthening extremism themselves. Let me—one thing about—you mentioned Prime Minister Maliki. Iraq is now experiencing the very detrimental and deadly effects of having Islamic extremists in—through ISIL and the other groups and now they are trying to counter them and it is disrupting the elections that are going on right now.

So, clearly, like as you say there is a real cost to Iraq that I think the prime minister recognizes and should recognize. Let me also say that we have been categorical with Prime Minister Maliki that Iraq needs to do its utmost to stop Iranian assistance from coming through Iraq to Syria and much more needs to be done on that score and we will continue pressing him. Thank you.

Ms. ROS-LEHTINEN. Thank you, Mr. Higgins.

Mr. Weber of Texas.

Mr. WEBER. Thank you. Questions on three fronts and we will probably start with you, Mr. Silverman. What would you say are the top—we are going to be short on time so I am going to say top two needs for the military, for the refugees and then the government? What are those top two needs for each of those three groups, and maybe Dr. Spence ought to address the military but how do—

and then what are the—what is your answer—the top two needs of refugees and the government?

Mr. SILVERMAN. For the refugees, Congressman, thank you, it is that strong international support that prevents the refugees from becoming any more of a political issue than it is now.

You have to deal with the demands. You know, Lebanese face competition in jobs, competition in rents, competition in all kinds of ways from the refugees. So we need to focus more on the host communities and building up the host communities. We are trying to do that.

Mr. WEBER. And, obviously, that is housing and water and jobs?

Mr. SILVERMAN. Water, educational facilities.

Mr. WEBER. And are we getting a lot of international support or are we going most of it alone?

Mr. SILVERMAN. You know, Congressman, I was in Kuwait with Secretary Kerry at the last donors conference for the Syrian conflict. It raised a record of $2.6 billion in pledges but until a couple of weeks ago I think the figure was 14 percent of those pledges have been delivered. Now the Kuwaitis, I understand, delivered some $¼ billion yesterday or the day before but just within recent days and that is a good thing, obviously.

Mr. WEBER. Okay.

Mr. SILVERMAN. But we need to have that follow-up.

Mr. WEBER. And the government—how do we assist the government?

Mr. SILVERMAN. I think we assist the government by assisting those responsible forces by calling for elections on time by the constitution and trying to prevent outside interference in the selection of leaders.

Mr. WEBER. Are we hated over there?

Mr. SILVERMAN. No, not by any means.

Mr. WEBER. Not by any means.

Mr. SILVERMAN. Not by any means, Congressman. No.

Mr. WEBER. So us getting involved is going to be a good thing categorically across the board?

Mr. SILVERMAN. I believe that the Lebanese people value very much value—I know the LAF values it but I think across Lebanese society there are many, many strong ties to this country, as you know.

Mr. WEBER. But, obviously, not so with the Hezbollah parts of the government. Let me just ask you a specific question. In June 2000, the U.N. certified that Israelis had withdrawn and all the Lebanese territory had been given back. But in August 2000, Lebanon's new cabinet approved a draft policy statements securing Hezbollah's existence as an armed organization and their guaranteed right to fight to remove Israeli occupation. Is that still their policy?

Mr. SILVERMAN. Congressman, I mentioned this ministerial statement that the government finally agreed on which allowed it to get its vote of confidence. In previous governments there had been language which talks about a government endorsement of the army, the people and the resistance, and everybody knew what the term ''the resistance'' means—Hezbollah.

Mr. WEBER. And so that is still in play?

Mr. SILVERMAN. No, no, no. That is out now. Under this new ministerial statement it now——

Mr. WEBER. Okay. When did that take place? I missed that.

Mr. SILVERMAN. That was just within the last month.

Mr. WEBER. Okay. And I am sorry. I am running out of time. Let me go over here to Dr. Spence.

Military—what is your suggestion?

Mr. SPENCE. You asked—Congressman, I would say there are two that you asked for. One would be border security and the other would be counterterrorism.

Mr. WEBER. But with all due respect, Dr. Spence, we can't even secure our own borders.

Mr. SPENCE. Well, I think—I think looking at this situation it is all the more reason we just need to do as much as we can to help the Lebanese Armed Forces secure their borders and I think it is through the 1206 program that we can try to do—that could try to do this.

Some of the equipment that we give to surveille the border, which is very, very porous, includes radars and sensors. And I think in these very difficult times to continue that support is important, and then also for the for-military financing to continue what we are doing for training, for vehicles, for helicopters, for communications.

Mr. WEBER. How do we ensure that none of those funds/equipment are falling into the hands of Hezbollah?

Mr. SPENCE. I think we need to continue the end use monitoring that we have, which is a critical part of our strategy to support the LAF as well as to counter Hezbollah.

Mr. WEBER. Are you aware of any of that making its way to Hezbollah currently or in the past?

Mr. SPENCE. I think right now, as we said, making sure that we limit the role of any of this equipment ending in—or training in this area.

Mr. WEBER. But that is not my question. Are you aware of any of it having fallen into the hands of Hezbollah in the past?

Mr. SPENCE. I think right now, Congressman, as I said, as we look at it very carefully. We want to make sure to engage senior Lebanese officials at a very robust level so we have good lines of communication.

Mr. WEBER. Is that a no?

Mr. SPENCE. Right now it is an answer that it is an ongoing something that we look at. As far as the end use monitoring that we have, having reviewed it carefully both on its own right and then as a result of the GAO report, I feel confident and good about our end use monitoring issues right now and we continue——

Mr. WEBER. You may feel confident and good but a lot of people are still getting killed. So that is why I want to make sure that nothing winds up in the hands of terrorists. Madam Chair, I yield back.

Ms. ROS-LEHTINEN. Thank you so much, Mr. Weber. Mr. Vargas of California.

Mr. VARGAS. Thank you very much, Madam Chair. I appreciate it. You know, one of the things I think is hard is for Americans to keep score here in Lebanon—who is where and what. I mean, the reality is that I think most Americans remember Beirut as the Paris of the Middle East and a wonderful place.

Then there was the civil war and then there was all sorts of conflict and then they were dragged in, and now there are extremists and now supposedly they like us again.

But I guess the general question I would ask is a question I think you began to answer. I would like you to expand. I mean, I think we shouldn't leave the field—I think it would be a mistake—because of extremists but I think a lot of Americans just said to hell with it. You know, why are we there—why are we spending money—why are we helping these guys.

I mean, at the end of the day we can't even keep score. Why should we be there, Mr. Silverman?

Mr. SILVERMAN. Congressman, thank you. I mean, I think your point on keeping score why it is so confusing, there are so many different factions and groups. That is exactly it.

It is a mosaic that needs to be protected. It is a pluralistic system that needs to be protected. It is a multi religious place which has leadership in the various branches that represent all religions. That is why it is so important just for the stability of where it is but also as a kind of a lesson that this can work in the Middle East.

It is extremely important. So you don't have to know all the details about Lebanon and I agree, it can be really, really daunting to anybody from the outside.

May I just say one thing about the ministerial statement that I didn't say earlier? This is not the kind of ministerial statement that we would have drafted or not. It is a net improvement with its respect to talking about resistance. But, again, it is not what we sought or what we wanted but it is something better than what we had, just to clarify. Thank you.

Mr. VARGAS. No worries. Dr. Spence, you are a southern Californian. How would you explain it to the guys back home? I mean, they take a look at this and they say, you know, what the hell are we doing there?

Mr. SPENCE. I think when I do and sometimes I am actually asked this at home over the Thanksgiving table—you know, what are you doing, especially coming back from here. I think what happens in Lebanon is hugely important for a lot of reasons.

First, we owe something to the Lebanese people. These are people aspiring for democratic government for their society. They want to freely choose their leaders and to get that and get the dreams they trying to—looking for they need security, they need stability and they are deserving of that.

I think, second, that what happens in Lebanon doesn't stay in Lebanon, that there is an impact around the region and our closest allies and partners that border Lebanon are deeply impacted by what happens in Lebanon. So what happens in Lebanon matters much broader than what happens actually in the country.

And I think, third, there are enemies, like Iran, which are trying to do things in Lebanon that are against America's national interest, and the more that we can counter what Iran is trying to do anyplace around the world strengthens the hands of what we are trying to do against our enemies.

Mr. VARGAS. And that, of course, makes sense to me. But then how do you explain this? I mean, we say well, they want democracy—we ought to help them out—and then they cozy up to Hezbollah.

I mean, they cozy up to terrorist groups. They cozy up to these groups that, you know, are anathema to what we believe in and, again, that is hard to explain to the people back home why we are spending, you know, $1.7 billion, you know, for these guys that say yes, you know, we love America and Hezbollah.

Mr. SILVERMAN. Congressman, just to say that the political situation in Lebanon is unique. The responsible voices, moderate voices are trying to deal with it as best they can. That is exactly why, though.

Since Hezbollah has a role let us support the Lebanese people that do not want to see this role in Lebanon and do not want to see the country dragged into a foreign conflict and that is why we need to support these other voices.

It is the situation in Lebanon now but I think we are all dedicated and we really believe that we can make progress toward a better situation in Lebanon. It doesn't have to have this role.

Mr. VARGAS. Okay. Before I yield back, I would say that, you know, for someone like myself there is a very large Christian contingent in the country, a very important Christian—and it needs to be protected. It is one of the reasons I think we should be there.

The Mennonite Christians have been there a long time, the Orthodox, and so again I appreciate all your efforts. I just think we have to do a better job explaining it to the American people because the American people are getting tired and I think we have to do a better job of communicating that.

But thank you so much for being here and thank you for giving it your shot. Thank you.

Ms. ROS-LEHTINEN. Thank you very much, Mr. Vargas, and good answers, gentlemen. And so pleased to yield to Mr. Meadows, who will be shepherding the Hezbollah bill through this session. Mr. Meadows.

Mr. MEADOWS. Thank you, Madam Chairman, and thank each of you for your testimony. I want to follow up a little bit on where my friend and colleague from California because it gets to be a very difficult sell.

You know, he may think it is difficult in California. It is much more difficult in North Carolina, and so as we start to look at that it is really about making sure that we stand with our allies, that we create a safe and secure environment for the Lebanese people. But even beyond that, if we look at Hezbollah and their influence, speak to where they are showing up other than in Lebanon.

I mean, you know, there have been reports of Latin America, Canada, you know, Europe. Part of the difficulty as we see this terrorist organization is that in Europe some view them as a charitable organization.

You know, you start to look at the rhetoric that is very difficult for me to defend. So Mr. Silverman, I can see you are—you can comment on that.

Mr. SILVERMAN. Can I comment as a former resident of North Carolina?

Mr. MEADOWS. Yes, that is great. We will give you honorary Tarheel status today.

Mr. SILVERMAN. Thank you, Congressman. I think, obviously, the swathe that Hezbollah cuts is indeed wide. It is unfortunate that it took the attacks in Bulgaria, the attacks in the operations in Cyprus and elsewhere and then, of course, in Latin America but it is unfortunate that it took so long to get Europe to designate. But, again, as I told you it is—in our view it is an imperfect designation and in any event it needs to be implemented to its fullest extent.

So that is why we need to—we really need and we do have a very broad diplomatic effort both, let us say, foreign ministries to foreign ministries but interior ministries to interior ministries, counterterrorism people to counterterrorism people what is the legislation that you need to inhibit Hezbollah's ability to fund itself.

Of course, Hezbollah is getting a lot of money from Iran as well and I think our sanctions on Iran help with that. I will say, you know, you mentioned, you know, some of these charitable organizations. I mentioned to you that today Germany banned a group.

Mr. MEADOWS. Right.

Mr. SILVERMAN. The name of that group was the Orphan Children Project for Lebanon.

Mr. MEADOWS. Right.

Mr. SILVERMAN. So that will give you an idea of what was being—apparently allegedly was being used as a front.

Mr. MEADOWS. Well, in the sanction bill that we put forth we are trying to with a scalpel provide an additional tool without throwing a wide net to say okay, here is what we need to go after.

We need to designate Hezbollah in another way to give us the ability to go after them. With that kind of legislation any concerns that you have there in terms of hampering what is going on? Certainly, we don't want to get in the way of Ambassador Sherman or anything else that is going on. Any concerns that you would have there?

Mr. SILVERMAN. Congressman, thank you, and of course we share your sentiment fully about Hezbollah and that is why they were designated in 1995 as a foreign terrorist organization.

There have been multiple executive orders. They were designated in 2012, both Hezbollah as an organization and Mr. Nasrallah for providing material support to the Assad regime. We have blocked assets. We have criminalized U.S. interaction. We have alerted financial institutions, et cetera.

With respect to the legislation itself, it was introduced yesterday and we are examining it now in detail through the interagency process. So I can't offer you a view here right now and today but we will be coming back to you, obviously, with our views on the legislation about what more can be done as well.

But I think a lot of it has to do with implementing what—in addition, implementing what we have and not just us, of course. As I said, other countries as well, which do not have all of the legislation that—and measures that we have in place.

Mr. MEADOWS. Well, we tried to identify some of those holes that we have been seeing and, honestly, have been working on this since last July and have held off for a number of reasons. And so as we look at that I would be interested in your input. I want to close out with this last question.

There have been widespread reports. I just returned from the region where you have Hezbollah among the Lebanese people. It makes it very difficult to have a free society when you have this terrorist group infiltrating not only neighborhoods but many of them, perhaps the military, government throughout. I would like each of you if you could speak to that, and I would yield back.

Mr. SILVERMAN. Congressman, for my part I would just say this is exactly why we have to build up the other side of the equation in Lebanon and that is what we are trying to do. I don't believe—you know, I don't believe Lebanon wants—the Lebanese people, the great majority of Lebanese people want the kind of policies that Hezbollah is promoting and certainly not its terrorism, certainly not its adventurism in foreign conflicts in which they have no business being.

You know, the Lebanese people were very happy to see Syria and Syrian troops leave their territory and that is why we need to support those voices in Lebanon.

Mr. SPENCE. Congressman, the one thing I would add is it is an issue that we need to work around the world to continue to isolate the role of Hezbollah and it is something that we can do.

I am sorry—to isolate the role of Hezbollah, to encourage the role of what the Lebanese Armed Forces are doing. So we work to isolate Hezbollah around the world. We need to work with our partners in doing it because the United States can play an important role on this but it is not something that we can do alone.

Mr. MEADOWS. I appreciate the patience of the chair.

Ms. ROS-LEHTINEN. And thank you for your leadership, Mr. Meadows.

Dr. Yoho, another Florida colleague.

Mr. YOHO. Madam Chair, thank you. Gentlemen, I appreciate your testimony here. Let me ask you, that $1.7 billion, how long of a time span has that been that we have given that foreign aid?

Mr. SILVERMAN. Congressman, the $1.7 billion that I cited was for the Syrian refugee crisis entirely. That was the $1.7 billion that——

Mr. YOHO. What time period is that? Is that——

Mr. SILVERMAN. So that is since the conflict began in 2011——

Mr. YOHO. Okay.

Mr. SILVERMAN [continuing]. And it refers to assistance inside Syria for displaced people and also to all of the neighbors that have received refugees.

Mr. YOHO. All right. And Mr. Silverman, you were stating in your written statement that you stated the need to implement U.N. SCR 1701 which calls for the disarmament of all armed groups in Lebanon.

What is being done to do that and who is monitoring that? How is it being done and what have we accomplished as far as doing that?

Mr. SILVERMAN. Congressman, I think we can all agree here that not enough has been done, obviously, because Hezbollah has not been disarmed and that is why we are trying to build up both the Lebanese political system and its one national institution, the only party that should carry arms in Lebanon, which is the Lebanese Armed Forces.

But and this is brought up all the time. We use this international support group as an international institution to continue to push for the implementation of 1701. Obviously, sir, we are not there yet. But we——

Mr. YOHO. Okay. So in your opinion would you say the U.N. resolution to do that has not been very effective as of today?

Mr. SILVERMAN. It has not been implemented, obviously, and the Lebanese people I think want it implemented but it has not been implemented.

Mr. YOHO. Dr. Spence, do you want to weigh in on that?

Mr. SPENCE. I would add to what Mr. Silverman said.

Mr. YOHO. Okay. Well, that comes down to then the next question. What is the lifeblood of the substance that keeps Hezbollah a force in having so much power? Is it—where does the main source of their revenues come from?

Mr. SILVERMAN. Well, I think Iranian support is very important. You know, we have—in our various designations of Hezbollah we have talked about their other efforts around the world to garner funds and in some cases through criminal enterprises.

We have talked about that they have benefitted from narcotics trafficking over the years. So they do that. Let me also say outside of the funds, you know, that, for example, Hezbollah talks about its involvement in Syria is, for example, protecting Shi'a heritage. Of course, that is not the——

Mr. YOHO. Right.

Mr. SILVERMAN [continuing]. That is not what they are doing in Syria at all and I think people realize that.

Mr. YOHO. Okay. Let me move on to this. What would be the best way to stop or neuter that support for Hezbollah? We have tried sanctions on Iran and what I have seen is Hezbollah has grown. They have extended and gone over to the—you know, into this hemisphere.

They are spreading throughout South America. There are reports of them coming up through Central America, even infiltrating into America. With these tough sanctions on Iran they are still growing. What else can we do?

Mr. SILVERMAN. Well, I don't think we should just dismiss the fact that or dismiss an effort with Iran to get them to stop supporting Hezbollah. But we also need, as Deputy Assistant Secretary Spence mentioned, a full effort by all of our allies and very close coordination with each other all around the world to get at the financial—to get at the financial networks.

Mr. YOHO. Okay. Dr. Spence, you were talking about the end use monitoring of—I guess it is the armament they have. Who is doing that, how often is it done and what are the metrics to determine the effectiveness of that? Start with who is the one doing that.

Mr. SPENCE. Sure. The—within—for the end use monitoring it is with our country team within Lebanon who looks at what they are actually doing. As far as a little more on the metrics and how we do it and some more details, I think it is a very important question that we owe you a level of detail. If it is okay with you I would like to come back with you for—with some more detail——

Mr. YOHO. I would like that if you could do that because——

Mr. SPENCE [continuing]. As to what this is so we can lay it out in a little more precise detail.

Mr. YOHO. I think what I have here is we have given them $180 million worth of equipment recently in weaponry. How do we know, like Congressman Weber brought up, that it is staying where it is supposed to, it is being used for what it is supposed to be used?

And I think that is something that is very important that we follow up on that. If Iran is working against the peace and stability in Lebanon, what is the Middle East or the Islamic world doing to pressure Iran to stop to help promote peace in that area so that we can back down, you know, and people can live their life the way they want to over there? What is that whole Middle Eastern population doing to put pressure on Iran and say stop?

Mr. SPENCE. I think doing that is extremely important and I think what we made clear is Iran is having destabilizing activities around the region. You know, it is not just Iran's nuclear program. It is their support of groups like Hezbollah and terrorist groups.

So what we try to do is make sure that when groups like Hezbollah claim to speak for the Lebanese people and claim to speak for all of Lebanon and provide security, that is not true.

That is why we want to strengthen groups like the Lebanon forces that actually can provide for the security and stability of Lebanon and I think that is why it is important. Any strategy that we take cannot just be a United States unilateral strategy.

It is working closely with those partners who are in the region who are closest and are most directly impacted by it.

Mr. YOHO. My time is out. I yield back.

Mr. MEADOWS. I thank the gentleman from Florida and the chair recognizes the gentleman from Georgia, Mr. Collins.

Mr. COLLINS. Thank you, Mr. Chairman. I appreciate it.

I want to take just a little different tack but I think it is within the purview of what we are doing here. The current Israeli-Palestinian peace negotiations remind me of the Israeli-Lebanon relationship. Lebanon receives something for giving up nothing.

In 2000, the Israeli military withdrew from southern Lebanon. This led to an entrenchment of Islamist militants who hit Israelis' population centers and remain capable of doing so. In order to build good will within the region, time and time again Israel has ceded land under its control in exchange for little to nothing.

I feel the same is occurring with the current peace negotiations between Israel and Palestinian Authority. Over 10 months of negotiations and Israel has released three rounds of prisoners and the Palestinian Authority has gone to the U.N. and received non-member state status.

As with Lebanon, Israel is giving up real concrete concessions while other negotiating body is asking to give up little. Earlier this year, it appears Secretary Kerry implied that if Israel failed in its negotiations with the Palestinian Authority, Israel could suffer an economic boycott.

What I want to know what other concrete concessions is Secretary Kerry prepared to propose to the Palestinian Authority in order to make the negotiations balanced. Mr. Silverman.

Mr. SILVERMAN. Thank you, Congressman. First, on your point about Secretary Kerry's remarks, and we said this at the time, that we really thought that they were taken very much out of context because actually what the Secretary was saying and restating was our absolutely opposition to what they call kind of the delegitimization of Israel around the world including boycotts and other resolutions, and we are totally opposed to any kind of boycotting or steps against Israel.

Mr. COLLINS. In some ways could the Secretary not be also delegitimizing Israel in the sense of the way we always seem to ask Israel for the concessions, they give the concessions and we get nothing in return? Are we not being an enabler at that point?

Mr. SILVERMAN. I don't—with respect to, Congressman, I don't agree that we have been an enabler. This is a negotiation between two parties and I will say that we were disappointed, obviously, most recently by the Palestinian signing of these applications to join conventions.

I have to say also we expressed disappointment on both sides too and that gets at the settlements issue. But I think we are—in effect our efforts at the peace process are not only to have a result that is a Palestinian state alongside a secure Israeli state but also that the Palestinians are obviously part of a process that we think in the end will help secure Israel further. We believe that.

Mr. COLLINS. Well, I think—look, expressing disappointment and also seeing one side continually and, in my opinion, and others give is really a hollow gesture in a sense.

Are they—and very quickly because I—but you can answer this. I want to—will any concessions be asked of the Palestinian Authority in the framework document that is designed to bring up the final negotiations to the peace? Are they being asked to do anything here?

Mr. SILVERMAN. Well, I think, Congressman, that they are being asked to come to an agreement with Israel on land. Obviously, they are being asked to come to an agreement on the status of refugees and the so-called, you know, and the right of return.

They are being asked on a whole series of issues that they are going to have to be, you know, difficult decisions and compromises made as part of this process. Let me just add, I mean, that this is not in the end a U.S. solution. These are negotiations between the parties in which they are still engaged literally as we speak there on the ground and they will either come to an agreement or they won't come to a mutual agreement.

Mr. COLLINS. That is understood and a given. I think the issue here is the U.S.' role and are we taking a very strong ally in Israel and working with the Palestinians. Are we basically saying Israel, you are going to have to do and the other is not. That is the problem I am having at this point. It seems like we are taking an ally and making them give and really not giving the Palestinian side.

Mr. SILVERMAN. Congressman, I think throughout this process and over many years we have been extremely sensitive to in trying to promote the security of Israel including through these negotiations, in addition to all the other bilateral steps we take for Israel.

Mr. COLLINS. Okay, I will accept that. At this point, I do want to change questions. You made a part and you said earlier the administration doing—you know, I want to know what the administration is doing in talks with Tehran to stop the Iranian weapons supply and, you know, to Hezbollah and if it is not, addressing it.

You said that you had expressed it but that is not really part of the nuclear talks and my question is is why not because many of us actually on this committee and others believe that the plan that was put in place actually encouraged them to continue their work in Syria while, you know, sort of focusing attention to the nuclear conflict. Why should this not be a part?

Mr. SILVERMAN. Congressman, thank you. I think that we have made absolutely crystal clear to Iran, to Tehran our opposition and our—and that we want to see Iran's sponsorship of terrorism and its active efforts to destabilize the region ended. So I think that has been made crystal clear to the leadership in Iran for many years.

This negotiation is focused on trying to get this nuclear agreement. But let me be clear that that is one part of the Iran issue for us, only one part of the Iran issue for us, and that all of the other behavior that we have seen, the policies and the actions that we have seen from Iran that are unacceptable remain on the table and we will be pressing and we are pressing these issues.

Mr. COLLINS. Well, as one member who believes that sanctions work not only in Iran, it was working and should have been left in—Hezbollah is the same way. We have got to do more, the European allies. As someone also in the military this is a nonmilitary step that we can do to actually control this.

My time is out. Madam Chair, I will yield back.

Ms. ROS-LEHTINEN. Thank you very much. Thank you. Mr. Connolly is recognized.

Mr. CONNOLLY. Thank you, Madam Chairman, and thank you to our panel for being here. Mr. Silverman, how would you describe the U.S. interest in Lebanon? What is our interest?

Mr. SILVERMAN. Most briefly, we have an interest, Congressman, in the stability, security and sovereignty of a democratic Lebanon with an open economy.

It is—obviously geographically it is absolutely critical to the larger stability in the Levant and the region, and a pluralistic democracy, I should add, because in some senses Lebanon is unique in the region.

Mr. CONNOLLY. Do you think that describes Lebanon today?

Mr. SILVERMAN. I think that there are threats to Lebanon's stability. There are threats to its security and——

Mr. CONNOLLY. Yes, but would you see it, for example, as an open and pluralistic democratic——

Mr. SILVERMAN. I think that it has a, obviously, a pluralistic population but I don't think the Lebanese would be satisfied with it as a democracy or as a—you know, we have had a long time here without the Parliament in session, for example. So that is clear to the Lebanese people too that they want a more active functioning democracy.

Mr. CONNOLLY. How would you describe the role of UNIFIL in trying to bolster that stability and security you talk about?

Mr. SILVERMAN. I think that, obviously, we are supportive of UNIFIL and the, roughly, 11,000 forces that it has there. I think that it has really helped prevent a situation, imperfect as it is, and we still have border incidents, obviously.

But I think the situation would be much worse without UNIFIL. And let me add that UNIFIL does what it does in very close cooperation with the LAF and the LAF has benefitted from training with UNIFIL.

So, again, we are not talking about a perfect situation but when we think about the security of Israel and we think about stability on the border, while it is not perfect it is better than it would be otherwise if UNIFIL had not been there.

Mr. CONNOLLY. Dr. Spence, how would you describe the coherence of the Lebanese military and its capability? And let me just say I have been involved with Lebanon for 30-something years and we have had several episodes where we thought we put back together the Lebanese military only to see it splinter along sectional lines, very tragically.

So what is different today, from your point of view, and do you think U.S. military assistance has made any kind of appreciable difference? I know you get paid to say of course it has so we will stipulate you believe, of course, it has. But qualitatively when you look at it, is it producing the results we hoped for?

Mr. SPENCE. Okay. I actually feel that way as well so it works out well. Look, I think that as you know well our goal for the Lebanese Armed Forces—it has been our goal for a while and it is our goal right now is to make sure that it continues to be the sole legitimate force within Lebanon to provide for the security and stability of the Lebanese people.

You know, what that does then it makes sure that the LAF is a lot stronger than Hezbollah and also that it can defend the threats to the state of Lebanon, which are enormous and are only increasing.

Right now, I feel like the U.S. assistance has made a concrete and important role and there are a few specific things that I would say now that at least that I think about because this is an issue that really keeps me up at night about what we can do to increase this support more and help make the LAF to be more effective.

For example, there are two things from last week that I would point out. Just last week, the Lebanese Armed Forces arrested 14 Syrians at a border checkpoint. Now, these Syrians were trying to come in to Lebanon.

They were carrying fake Lebanese IDs as well as military equipment, and as you know well, Congressman, the issue of the border is hugely important. So the more we can do to help them address that—the border is long, there is a lot more to go. That is an important step.

The second thing that also happened last week is the Lebanese Armed Forces captured a car bomb that was trying to pass through a security checkpoint in the Bekaa Valley. Again, these car bombs, when they are able to flow through freely, cause enormous destruction and terror within Lebanon and there is more that we are trying to do. So——

Mr. CONNOLLY. Dr. Spence, thank you for those examples. I have 35 seconds and the—oh, all right. Thank you, Madam Chairman.

What about the coherence issue though? I mean, is the Lebanese Armed Forces or are the Lebanese Armed Forces a coherent whole in contra distinction to past decades when they fell apart along sectional lines?

Mr. SPENCE. Right now as far as the trend lines go they are facing enormous pressure. But I think our assessment is that the coherence is working a positive direction. We think that part of it is due to the leadership and bravery of the leaders of Lebanese Armed Forces and that is where credit is due.

But also we think along the way our partnerships and training have been able to help reinforce what they are doing. That is our IMET programs. That is our FMF and, frankly, that is the senior and ongoing organizational contacts that we have between the United States military and the Lebanese Armed Forces.

Mr. CONNOLLY. And if the chair will allow just one ancillary question, with respect to this subject, Saudi Arabia has committed $3 billion—that is a lot—in military aid to a small country, Lebanon.

Can you just tell us how does that augment or contradict what we are trying to achieve in Lebanon in terms of building up a coherent national armed force to protect the sovereignty of the country, or does it?

Mr. SPENCE. I think on that and that grant was announced actually before I was in Lebanon in January so it is something we are focused on. First of all, I would say it does not decrease the need for United States assistance to the Lebanese Armed Forces.

The needs are significant and there is really no substitute for the power and quality of American military training around the world.

Mr. CONNOLLY. But does the $3 billion—is it the United States' point of view that this is a helpful augmentation of what we have been trying to do or is it sort of a sideshow that we are going to have to now manage?

Mr. SPENCE. So we think that more support for the Lebanese Armed Forces is better and it depends on how it is managed, and that is the reason that Larry and I actually are going to France later this month to have discussions with the French of exactly how it will be used and how do we make sure that we are all pulling on the same oar with respect to the assistance.

Mr. CONNOLLY. Mr. Silverman.

Mr. SILVERMAN. May I just add, as I mentioned earlier in the hearing on Thursday I will be in Rome with this international support group and that is our message. The assistance has to be complementary to it. It is what the Lebanese Armed Forces needs. It is not what people want to give them.

Mr. CONNOLLY. Yes. Thank you both very much, and Madam Chairman, thank you for your indulgence.

Ms. ROS-LEHTINEN. Thank you, Mr. Connolly. Excellent questions. And we are so grateful for your presence. Thank you for your testimony, and with that the subcommittee is adjourned.

Thank you, gentlemen.

[Whereupon, at 11:41 a.m. the committee was adjourned.]

APPENDIX

SUBCOMMITTEE HEARING NOTICE
COMMITTEE ON FOREIGN AFFAIRS
U.S. HOUSE OF REPRESENTATIVES
WASHINGTON, DC 20515-6128

Subcommittee on the Middle East and North Africa
Ileana Ros-Lehtinen (R-FL), Chairman

April 1, 2014

TO: MEMBERS OF THE COMMITTEE ON FOREIGN AFFAIRS

You are respectfully requested to attend an OPEN hearing of the Committee on Foreign Affairs to be held by the Subcommittee on the Middle East and North Africa, in Room 2172 of the Rayburn House Office Building (and available live on the Committee website at www.foreignaffairs.house.gov):

DATE: Tuesday, April 8, 2014

TIME: 10:00 a.m.

SUBJECT: Lebanon's Security Challenges and U.S. Interests

WITNESSES: Mr. Lawrence Silverman
                    Deputy Assistant Secretary
                    Bureau of Near Eastern Affairs
                    U.S. Department of State

                    Matthew Spence, Ph.D.
                    Deputy Assistant Secretary of Defense for Middle East Policy
                    U.S. Department of Defense

By Direction of the Chairman

The Committee on Foreign Affairs seeks to make its facilities accessible to persons with disabilities. If you are in need of special accommodations, please call 202/225-5021 at least four business days in advance of the event, whenever practicable. Questions with regard to special accommodations in general (including availability of Committee materials in alternative formats and assistive listening devices) may be directed to the Committee.

COMMITTEE ON FOREIGN AFFAIRS

MINUTES OF SUBCOMMITTEE ON _____ *Middle East and North Africa* _____ HEARING

Day___ *Tuesday*___ Date_____ *04/08/2014*___ Room_____ *2172*_____

Starting Time ___ *10:01 a.m.*___ Ending Time ___ *11:40 a.m.*___

Recesses _____ (____ to ____) (____ to ____) (____ to ____) (____ to ____) (____ to ____) (____ to ____)

Presiding Member(s)

Chairman Ros-Lehtinen, Rep. Meadows

Check all of the following that apply:

Open Session ☑
Executive (closed) Session ☐
Televised ☑

Electronically Recorded (taped) ☑
Stenographic Record ☑

TITLE OF HEARING:

Lebanon's Security Challenges and U.S. Interests

SUBCOMMITTEE MEMBERS PRESENT:

(See attendance sheet)

NON-SUBCOMMITTEE MEMBERS PRESENT: *(Mark with an * if they are not members of full committee.)*

None

HEARING WITNESSES: Same as meeting notice attached? Yes ☑ No ☐
(If "no", please list below and include title, agency, department, or organization.)

STATEMENTS FOR THE RECORD: *(List any statements submitted for the record.)*

None

TIME SCHEDULED TO RECONVENE _____
or
TIME ADJOURNED ___ *11:40 a.m.*___

Subcommittee Staff Director

56

Hearing Attendance

<u>Hearing Title</u>: Lebanon's Security Challenges and U.S. Interests

<u>Date</u>: 04/08/2014

Noncommittee Members

Member	Present
Ros-Lehtinen, Ileana (FL)	X
Chabot, Steve (OH)	X
Wilson, Joe (SC)	
Kinzinger, Adam (IL)	X
Cotton, Tom (AR)	X
Weber, Randy (TX)	X
Desantis, Ron (FL)	
Collins, Doug (GA)	X
Meadows, Mark (NC)	X
Yoho, Ted (FL)	X
Messer, Luke (IN)	X

Member	Present
Deutch, Ted (FL)	X
Connolly, Gerald (VA)	X
Higgins, Brian (NY)	X
Cicilline, David (RI)	
Grayson, Alan (FL)	
Vargas, Juan (CA)	X
Schneider, Bradley (IL)	X
Kennedy, Joseph (MA)	X
Meng, Grace (NY)	
Frankel, Lois (FL)